SUNWARD I'VE CLIMBED

HIGH FLIGHT

by John Gillespie Magee, Jr.

Oh, I have slipped the surly bonds of earth
   And danced the skies on laughter-silvered wings;
Sunward I've climbed, and joined the tumbling mirth
   Of sun-split clouds — and done a hundred things
You have not dreamed of — wheeled and soared and swung
   High in the sunlit silence. Hov'ring there,
I've chased the shouting wind along, and flung
   My eager craft through footless halls of air.
Up, up the long, delirious, burning blue
   I've topped the windswept heights with easy grace
Where never lark, or even eagle flew.
   And, while with silent, lifting mind I've trod
The high untrespassed sanctity of space,
   Put out my hand, and touched the face of God.

Official portrait which hangs in the Pentagon

Sunward I've Climbed

I've Climbed

A PERSONAL NARRATIVE
OF PEACE AND WAR

by

HOWARD A. CRAIG

Lieutenant General, USAF, Retired

TEXAS WESTERN PRESS
THE UNIVERSITY OF TEXAS AT EL PASO
1975

●

Edited by

DALE L. WALKER

●

Illustrations by

JOHN PAUL JONES

●

Library of Congress Catalog Card Number 74-80106
ISBN 0-87404-049-3

CHAPTERS

CHAPTERS (*Continued*)

To my wife, Rosalie
my daughter, Jeanne Stanfill
her husband, Dr. C. M. Stanfill
and my grandchildren, Craig, Nancy, and Suzanne

FOREWORD

In 1936, Cecil Lewis, in his splendid book SAGITTARIUS RISING, *pointed out the difficulty in writing an autobiography:*

"Within my study all is quiet and peaceful. The paper on which I write lies in a little pool of light, and my hand moves laboriously, back and across, back and across. Back and across the years! It is not easy. I kept no diary and memory, that imperfect, fragile vista of recorded thought, eludes and deceives. As in distorting mirrors at a fair, I can see myself long or stumpy, lean or fat, at will. Never my true self. Mercifully, no doubt.

"Still, I feel I can convey something after all. Not a connected narrative of adventure and heroism; rather, in a series of incidents and impressions, all that my mind remembers of the shape of things in all these years. Some of it perhaps will be inaccurate in detail, but broadly it is true. In case such things should be of interest before they escape me further, let me set them down."

Mr. Lewis, who flew combat patrols with the Royal Flying Corps in World War One, has said of his memoirs what I want to say about mine, and I cannot improve on his words.

El Paso, June 1, 1974   HOWARD A. CRAIG

SUNWARD I'VE CLIMBED

The Young Philadelphian

1910: Walter Brookins' Wonderful Flying Machine

IN THAT PART OF PHILADELPHIA where I grew it was
every family's ambition to spend part of the summer at "The
Shore," that is the beaches of New Jersey at Atlantic City.
If it could not be longer, a day or a weekend would have to suffice —
or maybe several during the long hot summer.

Our family was exceptionally fortunate in this ambition; I do not
remember a single summer that we did not spend at least a week on
the beach. In late spring, my parents took the train to Atlantic City
and rented a few rooms or a small cottage. The days on the beach were
halcyon days for youngsters, although one summer I got sunburned so
badly that I went to the hospital for a couple of days.

My aunt Kate and her husband C. B. Johnston bought a small hotel
on Atlantic Avenue in the Absecon section of the resort city in the late
summer of 1909. When school closed the next year, they invited me
and my sister Helen to visit there. We arrived about the 4th of July.
My aunt and uncle had remodeled the attic of their hotel into two large
rooms, each with a bath, and installed about six cots in each room.
Later in the summer, a group of our cousins arrived, filling the place
to capacity. It was a wonderful life. We spent our day on the beach and
returned to the hotel for the evening meal and sleep. I was 12 years old.

One morning shortly after we arrived, I was walking down the beach
toward Young's Million-Dollar Pier when I saw a group of young men
working on an apparatus which looked like a big box kite. A young
fellow with a checkered cap seemed to be the boss because he fussed
continually at the other men. Interested, I sat down on the sand and
watched them all morning. Several similar knots of helpers began as-

sembling more machinery and spreading it out on the beach. After lunching at the hotel, I returned to the "box kite" assembly area. Finally, toward evening, I could no longer restrain my curiosity: When the young man who seemed to be the boss passed near me, I asked him what kind of machine they were making. He said it was an *aeroplane,* a machine which could fly through the air, carrying a man, and if I wanted to see it fly, to come back tomorrow morning.

When I returned to the beach early the next day, I saw my checkered-cap friend and another man washing the aeroplane with sponges and buckets of fresh water. As soon as they were finished, I asked the boss why they had to wash their machine. He said the salty ocean spray was not good for it. In addition, they had to grease all the exposed metal parts of the aeroplane to prevent rust.

Checkered-cap and two other men then wheeled the machine to the crusted part of the sand formed by the high tide. Checkered-cap climbed into the machine and waited while the other two men manually turned the big "fan" until the engine started. After running the engine for a few minutes, Checkered-cap waved the men to release the wings. The machine moved slowly, gathered speed, and lifted itself into the air. The sight petrified me.

After circling over the beach, Checkered-cap descended and landed close to the take-off spot. He stopped the engine and, joined by his two helpers, moved the machine back up to its regular beach stall. He then came over to me and said, "Boy, how did you like that?" I was still so awestruck that I was unable to answer and stood there gawking. He laughed, patted me on the shoulder and walked away.

That night at dinner I tried to tell my uncle and aunt what a great thing I had witnessed. *A man actually had flown in an aeroplane!* But they did not seem to be impressed or very much interested in the event. My uncle said he had read about it in the newspaper. In those days I was not a newspaper reader but I soon got a copy of the evening paper — it might have been *The Atlantic Review* — and read the whole story. It told of the other aviators there — Glenn Curtiss† was one I remember and a fellow from Europe too. Atlantic City was sponsoring

† See Appendix I for capsule biographies.

an "Aviation Week," offering cash prizes for the fastest aeroplane, the one which flew highest, or landed closest to a mark on the beach; there were mimic battles between heavier-than-air machines and battleships (a decade or so later this would be a serious exercise) in which a prize of $1,000 was given to the first aviator to drop a bag of sand — representing a bomb — on the deck of the ship.

The city had set up a number of storage and service areas on the beach, furnishing each one with fresh water, and I was at my favorite place early the next morning to watch the men wash down their aeroplane. Presently my checkered-cap friend came over to me and said, "Do you want to help us clean up the machine?" Did I! He got me a bucket and a sponge and showed me what to do. When we had finished, three of us moved the machine to the well-packed part of the beach. Another man joined us.

After Checkered-cap climbed into the driver's seat the two men spun the fan until the engine started. Again he raced the engine while the two men held on to the wings. Satisfied that the engine was running well, Checkered-cap signaled them to let go and the machine inched forward, gathered momentum, and took to the air. This time it flew for about fifteen minutes before landing, and I heard the pilot tell the men he would take it up for altitude that afternoon. I stared at the machine in wonder: Could it go even higher than the seagulls?

My checkered-cap hero took off late in the day and climbed to a record height of 6,175 feet, winning a prize of $5,000. He accomplished his record by climbing his machine until he ran out of gasoline, and then spiraling down to a perfect landing with a dead engine. The newspaper made much of him: "His appearance was a signal for running applause when the crowds recognized the youth who has just attained his majority and who first appeared in the aviation field last April," *The Atlantic Review* story ran.

It was from the newspaper I first learned that my checkered-cap friend was Walter Brookins, "the Wright brothers' particular star," in the *Review's* words, "an aeroplanist whose rapid rise is considered one of the most noted achievements since the art came into existence. Almost a mere boy between 20 and 21 years of age, Brookins had never been in an aeroplane until as a pupil of the Wright brothers, he commenced his lessons less than three months ago."

When I was having dinner with the family on this memorable day, telling all who would listen to me what a nice person Mr. Brookins was and what a wonderful driver of his machine — in my view, he was the very best of everything — nobody around the hotel seemed to care.

The next morning, July 10, 1910, I was down on the beach very early but Mr. Brookins had arrived before me. Actually I believe he slept with his aeroplane. When we had finished the washing process and the greasing of all the metal parts, he asked me if I would like to take a ride up with him.

"You bet I would!" I said.

"Well, you get on home and bring me the written permission from your parents and I'll take you up."

I told him my parents were in Philadelphia and that I was living with my relatives but he said permission from my aunt and uncle would do.

I could not get back to the hotel fast enough. When I was able to get my aunt and uncle together, I told them of Mr. Brookins' offer to give me a ride if I had their consent. Uncle Charlie exploded — "Not in a thousand years! Are you crazy? What would your mother and father say if we allowed you to go up in one of those crazy flying machines? And what if you were killed?"

Heartbroken, I trudged back to tell Mr. Brookins the sad story. He said he was sorry and that I had been a big help to him, adding maybe someday I would have another chance to take a ride up.

The seed had been planted, and I resolved that I would never be content until I learned to fly.

The next day "Aviation Week" ended and the aeroplanes went their various ways — some flying, others being disassembled and shipped out by rail. My vacation also had drawn to a close, and it would soon be time to go back to Philadelphia and get ready for school.

I kept up with Mr. Brookins' exploits through the newspapers. He survived to be one of the few pioneer flyers to die a natural death. General Henry H. "Hap" Arnold, in his 1949 book *Global Mission*, tells the story that when he and General T. D. Milling of Louisiana were taking flying instructions from the Wright brothers in 1911, all were gathered in a hanger at Huffman Field near Dayton, Ohio, one rainy morning, drinking coffee and waiting for the weather to clear. The conversation got around to famous aviators and their accomplishments. During a lull, a young man spoke up and said that he didn't want to be the *best* aviator but the *oldest*. He became just about both, and he was my checkered-cap friend, Walter Brookins.

Walter Brookins

II

1914-18: Restlessness, Enlistment in Aviation

IN THE SUMMER OF 1914 I was stricken with a severe
case of appendicitis. I was taken to the Mary Drexel Annex
of the German Hospital in Philadelphia and operated on by
Dr. John B. Deaver, assisted by his brother Dr. Harry Deaver. These
two men had the reputation of being the foremost surgeons in Philadelphia at that time. However, I did not respond very well to their
postoperative treatment and failed to recover completely. It seems that
they were trying to have the inside of the incision heal before the outside. Every so often each week, I was taken to the operating room and
the outside incision was cauterized to keep it open and new drainage
tubes inserted — a terrible ordeal. After many weeks, my condition
became worse, and finally the doctors told my parents there was little
hope for my recovery. My parents decided to take me out of the hospital and down to Aunt Kate's hotel in Atlantic City. She arranged one
of her nicest rooms for me and sent for an old retired doctor who had
been their friend for many years.

He prescribed some medicine for me which he said would help to
heal the inside of the incisions and instructed that the bandages be left
on until he himself took them off. As I remember, they remained on
for about a week, and when they were removed, the incisions were
completely healed. Moreover, the medicine he had prescribed had healed the interior of the incisions, and in less than two weeks I was up
and walking around. I remained in Atlantic City until the end of September when the doctor said I was well enough to return to Philadelphia to reenter school.

This was my first year in high school and I could not seem to make
up for the loss of that month. I was especially troubled with mathe-

matics, but somehow managed to blunder through the first three years. One day in my fourth year however, my instructor in mathematics had a talk with me, saying in effect that he would not be able to graduate me because of my grades. I asked him what I should do, and he suggested that if I took special instructions at night, I might be able to complete the course satisfactorily. He mentioned several places where I could take this instruction, one of which was the old Franklin Institute on Seventh Street. It had a wonderful faculty of experienced teachers and a good reputation. So I enrolled, going to regular school in the daytime and special school at night. I had my hands full.

My restlessness increased. Finally I could stand it no longer. One morning early in the summer of 1916, I withdrew my savings from the bank and bought an excursion train ticket to Niagara Falls, without telling my parents. Arriving at the Falls, I crossed over the bridge and was immediately picked up by some Canadian soldiers and taken to their guard house, to stand accused of being a Canadian draft dodger. I explained to them that I was an American and if they wanted to verify it they could call my father in Philadelphia. The phone call proved my story and they let me go. Upon my return to Buffalo, close to flat broke, I decided to get a job on the Buffalo-Cleveland-Detroit passenger ship. All my first night I washed dishes and when we arrived in Cleveland in the early morning, I left the ship and hunted up Aunt Kate, who had moved to that city. Aghast, she said the police of the whole country were looking for me. She immediately got on the phone to my mother, took me to the railroad station, and bought me a ticket for Philadelphia. She waited until I was safely aboard and the train had departed.

When I arrived home, there was no scolding, no voice of criticism, no volley of "Why-did-you-do-this?" questions or anything else of that sort from my parents. To me this was a great lesson; they were hurt by this episode of waywardness but felt that any further discussion would just make matters worse.

I did not know what to do with myself and my parents were just as baffled. So I returned to double sessions of school. One evening in the spring of 1917, shortly after our country had entered the War in Europe, as I was leaving the Franklin Institute, I noticed a soldier sitting in the front hallway at a table littered and stacked with paper forms. He looked anxious to talk to someone so I spoke to him, asking what all the papers were about. He explained he was taking applications for the Aviation Section of the Army Signal Corps. Applicants would be enlisted as officer candidates, sent first to a ground school and then to a flying school and taught to fly.

When they completed this training, they would be commissioned first lieutenants in the Aviation Section of the Signal Corps. This all packed a special wallop for me; it carried me back to those days in Atlantic City with Mr. Brookins and the dreams that experience had generated in me. I told him I was interested and to let me have some of the applications. In a short time I had the forms completed and mailed them to Washington, D.C. I heard nothing from the War Department for about six months. In the meantime, I read in a Philadelphia newspaper that the Aviation Section of the Signal Corps of the U.S. Army was establishing a seaplane base near Essington, Pennsylvania, on the Delaware River a short distance below Philadelphia.

One Sunday afternoon, I decided to go down to see this place. The trolley car left me off about a mile from my destination. After walking awhile, I saw a small building on the edge of the river and a flying boat anchored off shore about a hundred yards. Being tired I started to short-cut across a newly planted lawn, when a voice called out to "go back and use the sidewalk," which I did. When I reached the porch of the small building, two men were standing there. One of them, a short, sandy-haired fellow, asked me what I wanted. I told him I wanted to learn to fly, and he then asked me from what college I had graduated. I said I had not graduated from any college. To this admission he replied emphatically that I did not have a chance of learning to fly. He said all flyers had to be officers and all officers had to be college graduates. He added that I *could* enlist as a mechanic. I felt like telling him that neither the Wright brothers nor Mr. Brookins had gone to college, but I let this thought pass, thanked him, and said I would look around some more. Many years later, I learned that this gentleman was Major (later General) Thomas DeWitt Milling and the other man was Captain William C. Ocker, whose home was not far from ours.

During the last part of this summer of 1917, I arranged with the admissions department of the University of Pennsylvania for entry into the Towne Scientific School, Pennsylvania's small engineering college, on a probationary basis, inasmuch as I expected to be called into active service any day. Before I had a chance to attend any classes, I received a letter from the War Department in response to my application, telling me to report for physical examination to the Aviation Examining Board at the University of Pennsylvania Hospital.

As I remember, ten of us took the examination. Eight men came from Lafayette College, near Easton, Pennsylvania, while Frank J. Dimond and I were from Philadelphia. Someone had told the Lafayette boys that one of the principal examination tests was "the spinning chair." In this test the doctor spun the subject's chair rapidly, stopped it, and asked the subject to point to a white, vertical line on the wall. He then reversed the turning movement, stopped and again asked the subject to point to the white line. These Lafayette fellows were perfect in pointing to the white line. The doctor then put me in the chair and spun it around. When he stopped and asked me to locate the white line, I pointed off to one side for a right hand spin and to the other side for a left hand spin. Frank Dimond's reaction was the same.

The examination completed, the doctor gathered us all together and told the Lafayette boys they were all disqualified. He said they had failed the spin test, confessing that he could not understand how all of them could be suffering from the same inner ear problem. Finally, one of the Lafayette boys spoke up and said that they had been told it was crucial to point to the white line so they had got a chair and practiced up on the spin test. The doctor had no mercy on them, but said he hoped that after a period of time their ears would be restored to health and then they might be given an opportunity to resubmit their applications.

Before we left the dispensary that evening, Frank Dimond and I were enlisted in the Aviation Section, Signal Reserve Corps, and told to go home and await further orders.

III

1917-18: *Cadetship at Princeton*

THE ORDERS ARRIVED during the last week in November,
1917, telling me to report to the School of Military Aeronautics at Princeton University on December 2. As I was saying goodbye to the family on that date, my grandfather Craig, who had
been ill, died suddenly in my arms. He had been a wheelwright, had
his own shop, and was a Methodist lay preacher. During the Civil War
he had been sent to Fort Monroe where his services as wheelwright
were badly needed. However, he fell ill and was discharged. Returning
to Philadelphia first, he went out to Minnesota as lay missionary but
was not successful in this line of work. Grandfather was always kind
and considerate with us children, constantly read his Bible, and died at
the age of 81 years.

In spite of our great grief and confusion over Grandfather's sudden
death, we decided I should continue my trip to Princeton. I met Frank
Dimond on the train, and the two of us were met by a truck at Princeton Junction.

The truck driver drove us to one of the dormitories and told us
where to report. When we entered the room, we saw sitting behind a
desk a middle-aged man in uniform with rows of ribbons on his chest.
After finding out who we were, he said he was Captain Braig. Years
later, at Langley Field, in Virginia, I got to know him better. He was
then a warrant officer, and I learned from him that he had served as a
sergeant of field artillery in Cuba and the Philippines during the Spanish-American War. After his return from the Philippines, he was stationed at West Point as First Sergeant of a field artillery battery. When
the World War came, he was commissioned in the Reserve as a 1st
lieutenant and then transferred to Princeton as Captain and Comman-

dant of Cadets. His full name was Eugene Braig, a fine person with a special understanding of young men.

He told us we would be assigned to Brown Hall, giving us the room number, which turned out to be on the top floor of this famous old dormitory. He then instructed us to go to the supply room, draw our equipment and get settled. Outside, we found our suitcases on the front steps and the truck gone. Picking up our bags, we asked a passing soldier for directions.

The supply sergeant hauled out mattresses, pillows, sheets, blankets, underwear, socks, shoes, shirts, and uniforms, a staggering pile of gear which we had to carry up four flights of stairs, making several trips. By supper time, both Frank Dimond and I were exhausted and hungry. We asked somebody when we could eat and were told that a bell would announce mealtime and that we had to be in uniform. We did not know which pieces of clothing fitted together, and we must have looked ridiculous as we went down to stand in ranks for supper call.

School started on December 2 and I think they wanted to give us a jolt at the outset by having us memorize all the parts of the Lewis machine gun, the functions of each part, stripping the gun and putting it back together in a certain time period, jams and how to clear them and so on. The air-cooled version of this Lewis gun was installed on all our aircraft overseas, having proved to be the most reliable machine gun then in use.

Leaving this class after an hour, we went into signaling where we learned to send and receive Morse Code faster and faster as the weeks went by. Then there was a class called "Aids to Flight," a beginner's course in air navigation. Our instructor was a young first lieutenant, very slim and sharp-looking, with wings embroidered on his jacket: an *aviator*, the first one we had seen at Princeton. Among many interesting things, he told us that an aeroplane always took off and landed into the wind. I remember asking him how a pilot knew the wind direction when he was aloft. A very good question, he said, explaining that if the pilot had to land at a place other than his home base he would have to watch for smoke being carried by the wind, or windmills, flags — sometimes even laundry drying on a clothesline.

We had instruction in aeroplanes, the theory of flight, engines, aerial observation for artillery spotting, and photography. For the first week though, our study concentrated on something called "Military Studies" — use of the principal paperwork of Army Administration, Army Regulations, Customs of the Service, guard mount and close order drill, signaling, and gunnery.

At the end of the first week, the Commandant, Major Dana H. Crissy (for whom Crissy Field near San Francisco was named) called a meeting of all the cadet students. This was the first time I had seen him. He too wore wings but with a little star above them — the insignia of a Junior Military Aviator which at that time was awarded only to Regular Army Officers who qualified as pilots. On his left sleeve Major Crissy wore a blue chevron, signifying three months war service in France.

He told us the Schools of Military Aeronautics at Georgia Tech, M. I. T. and Cornell were being closed and their student bodies transferred to Princeton. As facilities were not available to accommodate all the transferees at once, Major Crissy said he would like some of the Princeton students who lived less than a hundred miles away to volunteer to go home for two weeks, during which time he would be able to take care of the influx. It seemed to me that the weeks at home would provide an excellent opportunity to bone up on some of the subjects we were taking. I was terribly afraid I was going to fail in Signaling. (As it turned out, this was my best subject.)

Out of the several hundred cadets, about twenty-five men volunteered to go home — a poor showing, and I think the Commandant was disappointed. Still, Frank Dimond and I went back to Philadelphia together. During those weeks at home, I went downtown to Leary's Old Book Store and bought a copy of Page's *Airplane Engines* and a book on aeroplanes. I also bought a telegrapher's practice key to help me on my Signaling. When we returned to Princeton, we found that we had been dropped back one class. The training was three months long, and a class graduated every Saturday. My original date of graduation, March 2, would now be March 9, 1918.

The winter of 1917 - 1918 was probably the coldest and snowiest Princeton ever experienced. Snow banks six and seven feet high were ordinary and we had to dig through these drifts to the sidewalks. One night while I stood guard duty, walking along a deep-cut path, I saw a figure coming down the walk between the snow banks. I challenged him. He identified himself as the "Commanding General of the Eastern Department." I told him to advance and be recognized, and saw a rather heavy-set man with his muffler up around his ears. He had a small grey moustache and wore a military cap and a long military overcoat with wide black stripes around the cuff and two silver stars above the stripes. I looked at him and said, "Recognized, sir, pass on." For a moment, he hesitated, and I knew he wanted to ask me *how* I recognized him, but the cold was so bitter that he gave up the idea of starting a conversation and walked on. Shortly after this incident I was relieved of guard duty, and when I arrived at the guardhouse in the basement of Dodge Hall, I told the sergeant of the guard, one of the permanent detail at the school, of the encounter. He said, "My God, that was General Leonard Wood! I wonder if the Commandant knows he is on the post." He phoned Captain Braig and told him of the incident, and that was all I ever heard of the matter.

In those days Leonard Wood was a name to conjure with. He wore the Medal of Honor for his Indian Army days, commanded a brigade of cavalry (including the famous Rough Riders) in Cuba in the Spanish-American War, and was justly famous as a territorial governor in Cuba and later in the Philippines. He had been President McKinley's personal physician before he won fame with Theodore Roosevelt and the Rough Riders.

We had no vacation except for Christmas Day, working right through Christmas week with the tempo rising each hour, and some of our classmates falling by the wayside. We discovered this by noting the absence of certain names on the roster placed on the bulletin board each Monday morning.

Early in January, 1918, the Commandant called another meeting of the student body. He said apologetically that the War Department had decided that beginning immediately students who successfully finished the ground school and flying training would be commissioned 2nd lieutenants instead of 1st lieutenants, as stated in our original applications. A roar of indignation rose up from the students. As soon as things quieted down, Major Crissy again apologized but advised us to relax and accept it. He said he had another bad news announcement to make: The War Department had decided to change the pay of flying cadets who were candidates for a commission. Instead of receiving $100 per month and paying for our own rations, our pay would be reduced to $33 per month (the normal pay of a Private First Class, our actual rank) and the government would pay our rations. The Major said we could no longer hire waiters and dishwashers for our mess, and we would have to use service cooks and bakers. He added that it looked like the honeymoon was over, a fact that had already occurred to us, and he asked for volunteers to work in the mess hall for extra credit. In the event that insufficient volunteers reported to Captain Braig's office, students would be detailed by roster and no extra credit would be given.

Since I was having trouble with my studies at this time, I felt I needed all the additional credit I could get, so I volunteered for K.P. As I left the building, I met another cadet in our class, an older man by the name of Mooney, who had been in the Artillery before coming to ground school. He wore a red cord on his campaign hat denoting his previous specialty. He asked me if I had volunteered for K.P. and I said yes. He warned that K.P. stood for "kitchen police," something much worse than ordinary mess hall work. And he added the time-honored maxim, "Listen, kid, never volunteer for anything in this man's Army — they will stick you every time."

I worked in the kitchen for three weeks and while a roster system went into effect to rotate K.P. duty, it seemed a long time before my relief came around. These February days were very dismal ones for the cadets. The fact that they would be commissioned a rung lower than promised was a severe blow to morale. The mess, using service cooks and bakers, deteriorated fast.

We drilled in the basement of the main gymnasium and the drill instructor, an infantry officer, became a little provoked with my coming in late from K.P. duty. One morning he had all cadets lined up in a company front formation in the gym, standing at ease, when I arrived. He called out to me to take charge of the detachments. I was flabbergasted but managed to call out, "Squadrons attention!" This designation "squadrons" practically floored the officer in charge. He had been using the accepted term "company." All of us thought "squadrons" more appropriate. In any case, after I gave the commands "Right dress!" and "Count off!" the drill instructor told me to dismiss the troops. He probably had a sense of impending disaster if I continued much longer — and he was probably right.

My grades continued to deteriorate even though I studied more after I had been relieved of kitchen police. In my next to last week in school I received a notice to appear before the Academic Board: This would be the end, and I knew it.

On the Board sat President John Grier Hibben of the University; Major Crissy, Commandant of the School of Aeronautics; Captain Braig, Commandant of Cadets; and one or two civilian heads of the school departments. When I reported nervously to the group, President Hibben was very gentle, soft spoken and understanding. He said, "Mr. Craig, you appear to be having some difficulty with most of your studies. Your grades have been going down steadily. Is there anything we can do to help you?"

I ran through the list: volunteering to return home the previous December and the delay that caused me; the reduction in pay, the K.P., shortened study time before Taps, general frustration and low morale. But I added that if I could be permitted to remain in my present class for the next week, I felt I could show an improvement.

Major Crissy asked me, if the Board decided not to allow this extra week, if I would prefer to stay in the Army in some other line of work or to take my discharge. He warned that if I sought a discharge from the Army the draft would soon pick me up and I would have no choice of the branch of the service.

But, I told the Board, I had just passed my twentieth birthday and would not be eligible for a draft call for a year. Therefore, if necessary, I would take my discharge. I added that ever since I worked for Walter Brookins at Atlantic City in 1910, I had wanted to learn to fly, in fact, and it was my intention, if I received my discharge, to go directly to New York and enlist as an aviation cadet in the Canadian Royal Flying Corps.

Major Crissy's response was that if I took this action I would lose my citizenship as an American. I expressed regret at this but said firmly that I had volunteered my services to the United States, and if those services were not accepted, I would offer them elsewhere.

Captain Braig then interceded to remind the Board that I had stood forth twice when the Commandant requested volunteers, and that some favorable consideration should be given to this.

President Hibben closed the hearing by saying that I would be advised of the Board's decision. The next afternoon a notice was placed on the Bulletin Board permitting me to continue my classes. I did better in the following two weeks and graduated with the class of March 16, 1918. In a few days Special Order No. 52, dated March 22, 1918, The School of Military Aeronautics, Princeton University, New Jersey, was issued. It relieved us of duty at that station and ordered us to proceed on March 22, 1918, to the Aviation Concentration Camp, at Camp Dick, State Fair Grounds, Dallas, Texas.

Altogether there were forty-five of us. And we were going to fly!

Class of March 16, 1918, School of Military Aeronautics, Princeton University. Craig is top row (5); Frank Diamond is third row (27)

IV

1918: Camp Dick; Demerits in Dallas

✸ WE ARRIVED IN DALLAS on a wonderful Texas spring morning, the day warm and sunny without a cloud in the bright, blue sky; a welcome change from Princeton's dreadful weather.

Several trucks were waiting to take us to the State Fair Grounds where Camp Dick was located. When we arrived at the Administration Building, the truck master told us to leave our baggage in the trucks and he would take it to our "barracks." This turned out to be a building arranged with cattle stalls and I judged it had not been long since cattle had occupied the place. After we had checked into the Headquarters, our detachment leader marched us in formation down to the cattlepens. Our baggage was piled outside. In a few minutes a truck arrived stocked with shovels, hoes, rakes and water hoses, and we pitched in to clean up that part of the building we would occupy. This finished, we drew cots, mattresses, blankets and actually installed ourselves in the building, two men to a stall. Quite a bit of the bloom of Texas had rubbered off by this time. We just had time to shower and clean up before we had to fall out for retreat parade. Here we got the first sight of our squadron commander, a quiet spoken tall thin man with a small mustache. He wore a pair of wings which showed that he had already completed his flying training. His name was Oliver Gothlin, 1st Lieutenant. He did everything in his power to lighten our burdens in the weeks to come. In the middle twenties Oliver and I were to serve together at Luke Field in Hawaii. We could not understand why he had been sent to Camp Dick instead of overseas, but later we found the camp was a holding point for flying graduates as well as cadets.

We soon learned the principal activity at this camp was infantry drill and fatigue duty. There would be a formal parade at reveille, then breakfast followed by more infantry drill during the morning, and a formal guard mount just before lunch. After lunch, fatigue duty was followed by inspection inside and out of our "barracks," the parade ground and other areas within the camp. A delinquency (called a "demerit") by one man was charged against the whole squadron.

Each week a call would be made on the camp for the detail of so many men to flying schools. The Commanding Officer, a Colonel Steever, had devised a sytem of selecting these men from what he and his Adjutant, a Texan called Lieutenant Pennypacker, considered to be the best all-around squadron. A single delinquency by a single man in the squadron would of course rule that squadron out of selection for flying school. This system created much competition and deep resentment.

One day four or five of us were detailed to police along the fence surrounding the camp. After working hard for about two hours, the cadet in charge called a break. We sat down by the side of the road to rest, and in a few minutes Lieutenant Pennypacker came riding up on a horse and demanded to know what we were doing loafing there. One cadet tried to explain to him, but he took our names and said we would be given ten demerits each. The demerits were made official and our squadron was at the bottom of the list to move out for weeks. One demerit often kept a squadron from moving out to flying school and we had accumulated fifty in a few minutes time.

Most of the men believed the squadron which had been in camp longest should have been selected for flying school, and this system was later instituted.

Saturdays at Camp Dick were dreaded, for a ten-mile march with full pack was invariably scheduled on that day. I discovered on one of these marches that I had worn a hole in the sole of my shoe. During the remaining weeks at this awful place, I tried to get another pair of shoes without success. Another thing burned into my memory: Every morning for breakfast, except Sunday, we had stewed tomatoes, bread and coffee. It became almost impossible for me to enter the mess hall. If some classes or demonstrations in machine gunnery, map reading, navigation, aeroplanes and engines had been conducted, much more good would have come out of this place than whatever good resulted from the eternal drilling and fatigue. I think that someone had the idea that these exercises formed a good disciplinary measure — something proven true for ground troops, but having the opposite effect on airmen.

We rocked along week after week; it began to appear we would spend the rest of the war drilling in Dallas, Texas. Then one evening after retreat parade, Lieutenant Gothlin lined us up outside the barracks. He said a great need existed for aerial observers overseas, and anyone who would like to volunteer would receive a six-week course in aerial gunnery and bombing and then receive a commission as a second lieutenant and shipped overseas. "Volunteers will not receive pilot training," Lt. Gothlin added, "but anyone interested should report to my office after this formation." Most did not want to give up a crack at pilot training and decided to take their chances on getting out of Camp Dick some other way. I was so completely fed up with the place, I would have volunteered to be anything from grease-monkey to dishwasher to get out of there. Finally, it turned out that Frank Dimond and I were the only two volunteers chosen from our squadron. There were two or three from each of the other squadrons, and we made up a group of about twenty. The next day — this was early in May, 1918 — orders were published directing us to proceed to Selfridge Field, Michigan, for further training.

V

1918: Machineguns and Loops at Selfridge Field

⊛ UNTIL THE TIME WE ARRIVED, Selfridge had been a primary flying school. A considerable amount of construction was still going on, and mud was everywhere. The Commandant of Cadets was a heavy-set, jovial Irishman by the name of Captain Lanahan. The Field Commander was a flyer, Major Norman Jay Boots. He lived on a yacht moored to the seawall which surrounded two sides of the field. The vessel had been donated to Selfridge by a citizen of Detroit for the duration of the war.

The people at Selfridge apparently had not been told why we were there, and they assumed that we had been sent for pilot training. We did not enlighten them. We started on dual instruction, and several of our fellows had soloed before our real assignments were straightened out. But it was wonderful. Here I was really flying and with the wind in my face, ascending to the clouds — all my dreams were realized.

Then we started receiving some new "Jennies" — JN4-D and JN6-H aeroplanes which were modified for gunnery. The JN4-D was equipped with a 90 horsepower, eight-cylinder engine with overhead valves; the JN6-H was similar (except its engine was a Hispano-Suiza of 100-110 HP) and both were reliable machines.†

A ground range was constructed on an isolated spot on the reservation and an aerial gunnery range set up over Lake St. Clair.

Some of our class that I remember included the following cadets: Ralph Baskerville, Frank Dimond, Dudley Morrow, Daniel Morganthaler, Malcolm Moss, William H. Martin, Edward Westenhaver, William Fowler, John McDonough, Leon Truitt — and Howard Craig. We stayed together during the rest of the war.

† See Appendix II for airplane identifications.

As soon as the ranges were finished, we began training in earnest. There were not enough gunner-modified planes for all of us, so those who fired from the air in the morning would go to the ground range in the afternoon. The ground range had several different types of ground machine guns such as the Marlin, Browning, and Lewis.

All ground gunnery was under the direction of Captain Tracy Richardson of Missouri. He had a spectacular career behind him by then which included fighting as a machine gunner and soldier of fortune under many flags: Guatamala, Nicaragua, Mexico — together with exemplary service in World War I with the Canadian, British, and American forces.

The airplane had mounted over what had been the rear seat, a mechanism called a *tourelle* which held either one or two air-cooled Lewis machineguns. Our safety belts were attached to this tourelle. We stood up and by swinging our hips could rotate body and gun up to 360 degrees. The gun was mounted on a steel half-loop which extended across the tourelle and could be raised to the zenith or lowered to the base of the tourelle. Thus the gun could be made to cover the upper rear hemisphere of the plane and some of the lower hemisphere.

One day after we had expended all our ammunition on the targets at Lake St. Clair, my pilot turned around and shouted to me if I had ever done a loop. I told him no, so he said, "Here we go!" He climbed up to about 5000 feet and put the plane into a deep dive. I was standing up in the slipstream, holding the Lewis gun in one hand, the other in a death-grip on the tourelle. He started to pull up in a steep climb but did not have enough speed and stalled at the top of the loop, where I was upside down, hanging on my safety belt. The engine coughed a couple of times, and he kicked the plane off into a spin, which I am sure was unintentional. After a few turns he came out of the spin and headed for home. After we landed he asked me how I liked it. I told him I thought it was a lousy loop and I did not know whether the spin had been planned or not. He looked a little pained and said, "Well, I only have fifteen solo hours. What do you expect?"

The only military duty we had at Selfridge was standing guard, mainly for fire protection, and reporting breaks in the seawall. One night I had guard duty, walking the seawall, and shortly after midnight the corporal of the guard came out to my post with a telegram for me. He held the torch while I opened and read it, a message from my father congratulating me on receiving a commission as 2nd Lieutenant. I knew nothing about being commissioned nor did Captain Lanahan. I wired my father for the source of the information and it turned out that my name had been published along with a lot of others in the Philadelphia *Inquirer*. This news had us all excited. A few days later we received orders (still as cadets) to proceed to Mitchel Field, Long Island, New York.

Cadet at Camp Dick, Dallas, March 1918

VI

1918: Jennies, DeHavilands, AVROS at Mitchel Field

I WAS DESIGNATED to take charge of the detachment and
be responsible for their conduct and appearance. On arrival
at Mitchel, I lined the detachment up outside of Headquarters and then went in to report to the Adjutant who promptly blew his
stack wanting to know where we had been for the last ten days. He
and the War Department were searching all over for us. I told him
that we had come directly from Selfridge without delay. He said he
had held our commissions for almost a week and he swore us in on the
spot.

I reported to Major East, another Regular Army pilot with the star
above his wings and a blue chevron on his sleeve. He had a copy of our
commissioning order which he handed me, asking if I noticed anything
unusual in it. All the other cadets were listed in Air Service (A), I was
listed A.S.S.C. Major East said that "A.S.S.C." meant I was commissioned in the Regular Army and I would stay in the Army after the
war! After the war, I told the Major, I wanted to get out of the Army
as fast as I could and go back to school (the memories of Camp Dick
and infantry drill were still fresh in my mind). The order was apparently in error, Major East said, adding that if I had no objection, he
would notify the War Department. I had no objection.

In the mess hall that noon, I was the only one with the old white
band on my hat and enlisted man's insignia. All the others had dashed
to the Post Exchange to buy their gold bars, officer's hat cords and insignia.

There was a private room at each end of our barracks, evidently one
intended for the First Sergeant and the other for the Charge of Quarters. In one of these rooms there lived a white-haired Captain with a

whole string of ribbons on his chest. A veteran of the Spanish-American War, he was a big help to us. A few days after our arrival, I received an order making me "Summary Court Officer" for Mitchel Field. I had not the slightest idea what this meant, so I asked this veteran captain. From a shelf he took down a book entitled *The Manual of Courts Martial* and told me that I would find everything I needed to know in that book.

At Mitchel Field some new squadrons were being organized to fly DH4 (DeHaviland) airplanes. I was assigned to the 46th Aero Squadron and one day my pilot asked me to go with him out to the gun butts (earth made targets for aircraft machine gun practice) so he could sight the new forward-firing guns which had just been installed on the nose of his DH4. In a direct line with the butts was Camp Mills where ground troops were concentrated prior to debarkation overseas. We jacked the tail of the DH up in a level position and fired a few rounds from each gun at the target. I did not see any dust or movement of the target and neither did my pilot. Again we took careful aim and fired with the same results. He said something was wrong and we returned to the hanger. When we arrived at the hanger line, the place was in pandemonium. It seems that a company was lined up in a street at Camp Mills and suddenly bullets began to mow the men down (a few men were actually wounded). There is no doubt in my mind that it was our DH4, shooting over the butts, that caused the damage. However, the incident was put down as an accident and new butts built in another location.

After a few weeks at Mitchel, we were ordered over to Roosevelt Field near Mineola. A new squadron had just been organized there, the 352nd, to which I was assigned. Under the command of Captain Walter P. Jacob, all the pilots were very experienced for those days. This squadron, along with four or five others, formed The First Bombardment Expeditionary Wing. The Wing was commanded by Colonel Claude "Sunny" Rheinhart, and I saw him for the first time when he landed a new DH4 "Bluebird" on our field. This airplane was the handsomest I had ever seen: the fuselage painted a bright blue, the wings and tail surfaces their natural white linen color.

Captain Jacob put out a regular training schedule for camera obscura (bombing), camera gun and other gunnery training. He also scheduled cross-country flights for the pilots. One morning the whole squadron went down to Philadelphia in JN4-Ds and landed on the old Belmont Plateau. I called my father on the phone. A reporter standing nearby, unseen, took the whole conversation down and it was published in the newspaper the next day. We returned to Roosevelt Field that afternoon with no accidents. One of our flight commanders was 1st Lieutenant Roy Ludick whom I met again toward the end of World War II. He was then the AF Plant Representative at the Convair Plant, Ft. Worth, Texas, where they were building the B-36.

Among the fine pilots assigned to our squadron at Roosevelt Field, besides Jacob and Ludick, were Roberts, Lungren, Mullineaux, Griggs, Kirkpatrick, Coates, Wooley, and Forbes. If memory serves me, there were no serious accidents or casualties. Observers were not assigned to definite pilots, a practice which I think was a mistake, but I did most of my flying with Lieutenant Ludick. The training was conducted in a very serious and businesslike manner.

I still retained my designation as Summary Court Officer at Roosevelt Field, but the title meant nothing until the flu epidemic hit us in that summer of 1918. Then my troubles began. When a man died, it befell me as Summary Court Officer to make an inventory of all his personal belongings and place them in a warehouse for safekeeping until his next of kin told me what to do with them.

We lived two to four men in pyramidal tents and I think these four-man tents suffered the worst casualties. The boys died like flies, and I kept busy making inventories of their effects, meeting their people at the Long Island railroad station at Mineola, and making reservations for them at one of the Mineola hotels. I had trouble with only one mother. She said that she did not find the watch she had given her boy the past Christmas. Terribly distraught, she blamed everybody for everything, and she actually accused me of taking the watch. I told her there was a pawn ticket among the boy's effects and I would wager that, being near the end of the month and broke, he had pawned the watch. She was still not convinced when I took her and her husband back to the hotel. I then went through the boy's effects, located the pawn ticket, and took the train to New York. Locating the pawn shop,

I asked the proprietor to show me what had been pawned. He brought out a very handsome watch on which he had loaned $20.00. The next day I took the father down to New York, secured the watch and returned to Mineola. When he handed the watch to his wife, she was overjoyed and apologized to me most humbly.

Early in October one of the pilots asked me to go along with him to watch a demonstration at one of the outlying fields, Brinkley Field on Long Island. We flew over to find quite a delegation present: Royal Air Force officers, Canadians, U.S. flying officers and a small group of four or five cadets. On the flying line were three airplanes of a type I had never seen before. The pronounced hallmark was a long skid that extended forward between the wheels and below the arc of the propeller — this to prevent the aeroplane from nosing over. Otherwise the plane looked very much like the JN4-D. It was called an AVRO, a British primary trainer which flew similarly to our JN4-D.

A RAF officer explained to us that each of the cadets would take off, circle the field and land. They had had no dual instruction; in fact, they had never been in the air, but they had been "instructed thoroughly in the operation of all the controls." They would demonstrate how easily this British AVRO primary trainer would fly. The first cadet got in one of the planes and started the engine. After giving it time to warm up, he taxied out and pointed the plane into the wind, opened the throttle and took off. The take-off seemed rather ragged, but he finally got into the air and things smoothed out for him. He made some flat turns around the field before starting his approach to land. We could see immediately by the angle of his glide he was going to overshoot the field. About this time the cadet himself realized he was going to overshoot so he revved the engine while he was still about fifty feet in the air and started around again. His banks on the corners improved this time and when he started his glide in for a landing, it looked as if he was going to make it. However, probably thinking he would undershoot the field, he kept raising his nose and flattening his glide until, when he was about over the middle of the field, he lost flying speed and pancaked in from about twenty-five feet. He climbed out unhurt, but the plane was badly damaged. The next cadet pushed his stick too far forward and went over on his nose on the take-off. This machine was

almost completely washed out. Third cadet acted like a real professional, made a nice take off, circled the field, and came in for a perfect
landing. Fortunately, no one hurt seriously in the entire demonstration.

My pilot asked me what I thought of the demonstration. I told him
it was the craziest thing I ever heard of and it was just luck that no
one was killed. The British promoted this scheme as a great saver of
dual-instruction time, so we could turn out more pilots quicker, but I
think the real purpose of the demonstration was to sell us on the use
of the AVRO as a primary trainer. It was a good machine but, in my
opinion, no better than the JN4-D.

Also about this time, a New York woman's organization, designed,
I suppose, to aid and comfort aviators, sent word to Captain Jacob that
they had established a credit account at Abercombie and Fitch, the famous New York department store, so that any of his aviators could go
to the store and order any item of flying clothing they wanted. The
captain gave each of us a letter of identification and at first opportunity
we all charged down to the city to pick out some new flying clothes.
When we got down to the store there stood a committee from this
women's organization, all smiling beautifully, happy that they could do
something for their country and its fighting men. I picked myself a
heavy, fur-lined, teddy-bear flying suit, believing this would be just the
thing for standing up in the back seat of a DH4 during the cold, winter
weather — and it was. Our gang stripped the store clean of aviator
clothing — helmets, goggles, gloves, boots, the whole nine yards, and
I believe we thus became the best equipped outfit in the Army.

VII

1918-19: *Armistice! Taylor Field Training*

✦ AT THE END OF OCTOBER, the whole wing received orders to proceed to Hoboken for sea transportation to Europe. I think, due to Captain Jacob's efforts, we were the best-trained squadron scheduled to leave the U.S., both in flying personnel and mechanical and supply men. We went down to the Port individually and checked in, receiving an ID card and medical shots. As Frank Dimond and I had attended Princeton, we were invited to stay at the Princeton Club whenever we were in New York. This club, operated by the Alumni Association, had gone to great expense and trouble to fix the upper floor of the house as a dormitory, installing extra bathrooms. It was very pleasant with a fine restaurant which was not too expensive. Every day we all checked in with the port authorities with no sign of getting aboard the ship, although thousands of Doughboys were shipped out daily.

Then, on November 11, 1918, the Armistice was announced! Most of our gang was at the McAlpin Hotel and I think we stayed there during all the celebration. Malcolm Moss, a member of the group which had volunteered at Camp Dick for observer training, and I decided to take a walk up Broadway. Neither of us realized what a jam there would be in the streets, particularly Broadway.

Not getting to Europe for the War was a big disappointment to us all. Most of us wanted badly to get into the fighting and with the coming of peace, we found ourselves without plans for work or school. I did want to attend the University of Vermont in the worst way but I wanted to obtain my pilot's rating first. Malcolm Moss, upon announcement of the Armistice, said he wanted to get out of the service and I saw no more of him until I had duty in Hawaii. One night I saw him

at another table in a hotel dining room and after our reunion we kept
in touch with one another. In World War Two, Malcolm came back
on active service in the Intelligence Department. After the war he went
into business in San Francisco and died in the early 1960s.

But now we were on our way down Broadway. With no room to
walk abreast, Malcolm and I were separated in the cheering throng.
Finally I found a place outside of Keene's Chop House where I could
stand and not be squeezed to death while I watched the crowd go by.
A group of eight or ten people came along and tried to push into
Keene's. During the struggle one of the men came over to me and said,
"You look lonesome, soldier-boy. Come in and join us!" I did. They
had a private dining room reserved and all wanted to dance. Before
they left for the dance floor, one man ordered drinks for everybody,
including me. It was distinctly against the law to serve drinks to men
in uniform during the war, but everybody seemed to think that law
ended that night. About midnight I thanked the people in the party
and left, fighting my way back to the McAlpin in the crowd. I found
Malcolm asleep in one of the chairs in the lobby and both of us went
into the coffee shop and ordered a bowl of rice and a cup of tea.

The next day Fank Dimond and I went down to the Port together,
where several long lines of men stood waiting their turns to be inter-
viewed by officers sitting behind tables. When I got up before one of
them, he asked if I wanted to stay in the Army or take my discharge.
Those who wanted to get out received their discharge right there. I told
him I wanted to stay in because I still wanted to be a pilot. He said for
me to report again the following morning. That night we had a big
farewell party at the McAlpin.

The next morning, still elated from the Armistice celebration, I
checked in at Hoboken and there were orders for me to go to Taylor
Field in Montgomery, Alabama, upon any leave granted to me. Further
orders granted me ten days leave which I spent at home in Philadelphia.

When my leave ended, I caught the train for Montgomery, and the
porter kindly but mistakenly gave me the lower berth. About ten
o'clock at night, I piled into the berth and went sound asleep. In the
morning, while I was dressing, the man in the upper berth awoke and

we exchanged pleasantries. It turned out I had taken his lower berth. As he was getting into his blouse, I saw a pair of wings with the star over them and the silver leaves on the shoulder straps. He explained, "I am Colonel Seth Cook, assigned to the command of Taylor Field." I was terribly embarrassed having "ranked" my future boss out of his lower berth. I introduced myself, stating my hope that I could complete pilot training while at Taylor.

I believe that Col. Cook himself was instrumental in placing me in the RMA (Reserve Military Aviator) course, which I completed. He was primarily a cavalry officer and transferred to the Aviation Section of the Signal Corps in 1916 upon completing his flying training. He was a very approachable man and upon leaving Taylor Field, Alabama, was assigned to Chanute Field, Rantoul, Illinois, where he died.

Mrs. Cook and her two children arrived a week or so later. It was the first time I had seen a woman and children living on a military post. The Cooks were wonderful people. They took great interest in the four or five of us who were left at Taylor after the war. I still remember, on Easter day, 1919, they took us with them in the Commanding Officer's old official Cadillac on a trip up to Birmingham.

All the enlisted men were discharged at Taylor during the months of January, February, and March, 1919. They had become rather rebellious, and the C.O. had confined many of them to their barracks. I had been appointed Provost Marshal, in addition to several other jobs, and we saw them go with profound relief.

The spring rains started, and not long after several of the bridges between the Field and the city of Montgomery were washed out. This prevented the Quartermaster from bringing in supplies, especially food, as we had no railroad connection with the city. Colonel Cook told me to get some trucks, lumber and tools and take the remaining men in the barracks to repair the bridges. The men gave no trouble, and I gathered that they would rather be busy than sitting around their barracks doing nothing. We had completed the repair of one of the bridges and were starting on the second when two or three men rode up in a wagon. One announced, "I am the County Road Commissioner, and I want to know who gave you authority to do this work." I told him no one had given me authority, that it was just a plain necessity in order to get food to the base at Taylor Field. We saw nothing being done by the County to correct the situation so the Commanding Officer ordered me to go out and fix it up. "If you have anything further that you want to know, you had better see Colonel Cook," I told him. He never appeared again. We repaired all the bridges and culverts and graded the road for the whole eighteen miles from Taylor Field to the city.

After road building came flight training. Lieutenant Karl Guenther had been detailed as my instructor in flying. He was a fine man, short in stature, blond with very blue eyes, an excellent pilot and a splendid instructor, discerning, articulate and patient, an ideal teacher. We followed the training program step by step, and each step had to be completed to his satisfaction before we progressed to the next. I had great trouble with acrobatics — it just seemed I could not relax sufficiently — and this was especially true of barrel rolls. I did fairly well rolling to the right but had much difficulty with rolls to the left. We went over and over left-handed rolls until at last he said he thought I could get by. In June, 1919, Karl Guenther was transferred to Germany where he died in an accident a few months later, a great loss.

When Karl Guenther was not available, Leo Chase would take me up. A fine fellow from Janesville, Wisconsin, he was tall and slim, not a particularly handsome man because of his large hooked nose, but as genuine as they come. Leo was a Gosport instructor, one of the best. The Gosport system, which originated at an English flying school by that name, provided a two-way communication system in which a speaking tube was fitted into our helmets. Leo Chase could see some of the mistakes I was making in my flying and by talking to me through the speaking tube at the time they were happening, helped me overcome them.

Ken Fraser, who had been Officer-in-Charge of Flying when Taylor was a primary instruction school, gave me my final check-ride and, with a few suggestions for further improvement, recommended me for the RMA rating. Fraser had been an Arizona cowboy before entering the Army and spoke fluent Spanish.

Colonel Cook sent his recommendation to the Chief of Air Service Office, telling them I had completed the RMA course successfully and that I should be rated. The Chief's Office replied that they were not rating any more officers RMA, although I know many who received the rating at that time and later, men who did not have the thorough course of instruction that I had had.

This rejection came as a real blow to me but it was soon forgotten when the C.O. received orders for us to have all the JN4-DS dismantled and prepared for shipment to the Curtiss Company at Garden City, Long Island, New York. By this time all the enlisted men had been discharged or transferred to other stations, and only Colonel Cook and we four lieutenants remained. Colonel Cook called us together to say there was no use bucking this directive and we had better start in with the job. He joined us. Everyday we would go down to the hangars with our tool kits and work all day taking the Jennies apart. There must have been over a hundred of them. I learned airplane mechanics thoroughly.

*Lieutenant Howard A. Craig at
Hazelhurst Field, Mineola, Long
Island, October 15, 1918*

VIII

1919-20: *Field Artillery, A Civilian Again*

AFTER WORKING on the dismantling job for a couple of weeks, orders arrived one morning transferring Leo Chase and me to the Field Artillery and directing us to report, without delay, to the Commanding General, Camp Jackson, Columbia, South Carolina.

A few days later, Leo and I arrived at Camp Jackson where we were assigned to a horse-drawn battery of Field Artillery whose regiment had just returned from the Army of Occupation in Germany. Its officers had been through almost every campaign since we had entered the war in the spring of 1917. When we reported to the Captain of the Battery, he asked us if we knew anything about Field Artillery. "No." He then asked us if we could ride a horse. "No." He said he would set up a school for us, to give us all the fundamentals of Field Artillery with an hour each morning for equitation. We thanked him rather unhappily.

Our school was conducted by a 1st Lieutenant who certainly knew his Field Artillery. We started in with a short course in surveying, then the different kinds of artillery fire, how to regulate or adjust it, and how to maintain the guns. Our equitation course was conducted by the stable sergeant, also very competent, and after ten days we began to feel comfortable riding around the corral at a trot, canter, and gallop.

Nearly all the officers in this regiment were reservists, many of whom wanted to stay in the service. The principal topic of conservation at the club was the examinations for the Regular Army. All of them were taking a course of instruction in something or other. So it was a considerable surprise when orders arrived from the War Department directing the transfer of the whole regiment to the Philippines.

That night Leo and I had a long, soul-searching talk. It was my view that we did not stand a chance of getting into the Regular Army as Artillery men — the competition was too stiff. All these Field Artillery men had been through the entire war and probably knew the answer to every question from their war experience alone. And now that we were to go to the Philippines, where the examinations would be held, our chances were worse than ever. I said I intended to request my discharge. Leo said before we did anything drastic we ought to talk to the General who might give us some good advice.

The next day we got permission from the Battery Commander to see General Bell, who was a kindly gentleman with white hair and a white moustache. He finally said he thought we were right about the Regular Army examinations, that we would scarely have a chance of competing successfully and also that we were right in leaving the service. He said it was his experience over many years that our transfer was a typical pattern of the War Department and within a year or two they might be asking for officer candidates for Regular Army Air Service. He proved to be exactly right.

We left his office and asked the Adjutant whom we could see to obtain our discharge. This step was unbelievably simple, and by that evening Leo and I were out of the Army.

We went back to our quarters and Leo said, "What now?"

I said, "I'm going back to Philadelphia, but first I think I'll spend a few days at Atlantic City."

The idea appealed to him too. He said he had an offer from the Curtiss Company at Garden City to be a test pilot, and he thought he would take them up on it. So after a few days at the shore, Leo left for New York and I for Philadelphia. I saw Leo Chase once afterward in about 1933, when I had occasion to fly into the Buffalo Airport. He was airport manager.

In this hiatus between June, 1919, and early 1920, I worked hard at civilian life — managing an army surplus goods store and trying my hand as a junior aeronautical engineer at the Naval Aircraft factory, U.S. Navy Yard, in Philadelphia. I had hopes too of entering the University of Vermont, but in the spring of 1920 I received a letter from the Adjutant General of the Army asking me if I was still interested in a commission as 2nd Lieutenant in the Regular Army Air Service.

The chance to fly again took hold of me and I filled out the paper-work with anxious pleasure. Not even the prospect of having to take a week long examination — necessary since I had no college credits — could dampen my spirit.

To me, the exams were not too difficult. The last test was a 1500-word thesis or discussion on any aviation subject we might choose. I remember well that I selected as my subject "The Future of the Rigid Airship." In my enthusiasm, I fear I went overboard in estimating the potential of this type of aircraft. After we had completed our essay, we were called into a room where a board of officers sat. The only Air Service man on this Board was Major Fred L. Martin, a non-flyer. He asked me how many different types of airplanes I had flown, how I would execute a loop, a spin, an Immelmann turn,† what kind of engines did certain planes have, and so on. I thought I gave him pretty good answers, and when he finished questioning me, no one else had any questions.

I went back to my job in the Naval Aircraft factory and a period of long, painful waiting. Summer passed and autumn began, but finally, on 25 November, 1920, my appointment arrived and my orders to report to Camp Dix, New Jersey. I had to look two or three times to make sure that my commission was in the Air Service, because there was no aviation activity of any kind at Camp Dix. The next day I went down to the Aircraft factory and hunted up the legal officer who was authorized to swear me in. My boss, apparently very happy about my appointment, congratulated me and also Hill, a fellow plant worker who had also taken and passed the exams, and was also en route to Dix. He had seen service in France in the war.

I had no inkling of the future then, the events — trivial or important, sad or happy or simply astonishing — that would take me through a career in a new service to war, to high offices with distinguished men, to work with world leaders. These lay before me, but I lived in the present.

_____

† A maneuver in which an airplane first completes a half loop upward (to gain altitude), then a half roll to change direction 180°. Named for the German aviator Max Immelmann [1890-1916].

IX

1920: Camp Dix, Tea With General Summerall

THE ADJUTANT AT CAMP DIX was as confused as I regarding the reason I had been ordered there. Only the 1st Division was stationed in the camp and it had returned from Germany three months earlier. He assigned me a room in the Bachelor Officer's Quarters and gave me a duty assignment to Headquarters Troop, 1st Division. He said that the captain in command of the Troop had not had any leave since the Division returned from Germany, because there was no one to take over the Troop. My arrival would enable him to go home and see his family.

I walked to where the Troop was located, about a mile, and reported in to the C.O. He said, "At last, thank God! I am on my way. You can trust the First Sergeant with everything. But you take charge of all monies. Don't trust them to anyone." He dashed out of the room and that was the last I ever saw of him.

The First Sergeant introduced himself and asked me if I could ride. Thinking back to my Camp Jackson days with the Field Artillery battery, I told him "not very well." He said that the Commanding General, Charles P. Summerall, scheduled "Tactical Rides" every so often and that I would be expected to ride along with him to give the commands as directed by the General. If it was okay with me, he would have the stable sergeant give me some lessons. These continued every day, along with instructions in riding etiquette, stable inspections, nomenclature of the bridle and saddle. He was an excellent instructor. He also had me practice giving commands, which came in very handy.

The weather at Camp Dix at this time of the year was frightful. Often we would have a drizzling rain all day with a freezing sleet at night, making the roads treacherous and lives miserable. Pay day fell at the end of November, and each organization commander was required to go to the Finance Office and draw the pay for the troops. The roads were too slick for us to ride horses to the Finance Office, located in the center of the Camp, so we hitched up a buckboard with two mules. This caused a few lifted eyebrows around the Finance Office, but it bothered me not at all.

The next day the Commanding General scheduled a meeting of all commanders in the Post Theatre. I used the buckboard to go within a few blocks of the theatre and walked the rest of the distance. I took an aisle seat on the last row of the theatre, but I noticed that all the other officers took seats as far in front as they could get. Presently, General Summerall came out on the stage; whereupon everyone stood up until he told us to be seated. This stern, white haired old soldier then looked out over the theatre and spotted me in the last row. He shouted, "You back there, come up and take a seat in front." When I had settled myself in an empty seat in the first row, he looked down at me and asked, "Are you the new Division Air Officer?"

I replied "No, sir, I am the Commander of Headquarters Troop." He scowled at me and went on with the meeting.

I am afraid that the mention of Headquarters Troop reminded the old boy that he had not had a Tactical Ride in quite some time, because the next day a notice went around advising staff and command there would be such a ride the following Saturday morning at 8 o'clock, weather permitting. The First Sergeant advised me I would take the General's and Aide's mounts up to the General's quarters. All the other people who were to participate in the ride were lined up in a double rank along the street. When the General came out, I would hold the reins until he was mounted and then take my place on his left. I might say here that we had about 100 horses in our stable, most of them assigned to individuals. Presently, the General and his Aide came out of the quarters and I went through the protocol of mounting him up. He instructed me to have the others march in a column of twos, behind us. I gave the order loud and clear, and the old boy gave me a very searching look as our mounts paced down the road. Fortunately, the footing was good, and when we got outside the populated part of the Camp, we went through the trot, canter and gallop stages until the General decided to return. The old stable sergeant had really called the shots on the commands the old man had given me, and I think I came out of this first ride with some credit. The stable sergeant had made the ride with us and he came up to help me with the General and aide's horses. I don't believe I ever appreciated a compliment so much as when he told me I had done "real well."

Just before pay day, Hill reported in and immediately got himself in a peck of trouble. During the latter part of the War he had been detailed as a "Town Mayor" of some little French village. The job consisted mainly of resolving difficulties between the French civilians and the American military. In any case, Hill, back in active service again, now wore a uniform consisting of beautiful Bedford cord English-made breeches, Peale boots and an old style Royal Flying Corps (not Royal Air Force) double-breasted woolen jacket, with American insignia and wings on it, complete with the RAF overseas cap.

The Adjutant nearly blew a fuse when he first saw this getup and ordered Hill to get into an American blouse and cap forthwith. Hill lit out posthaste for the tailor shop and a few hours later reported back to the Adjutant, looking a bit more like an American than a British aviator.

One weekend one of the fellows in the BOQ suggested that several of us go up to New York for dinner and a show. This sounded good to me. We would leave on Saturday afternoon and return Sunday evening. On Saturday morning I went down to the orderly room and there found a written invitation saying that General and Mrs. Summerall cordially invited Lieutenant Craig for tea at their quarters on Sunday afternoon, from 4-6 p.m. I did not pay much attention to it because of the New York trip, but Monday morning I received a call saying the Genearl wanted to see me right away. I asked the 1st Sergeant to have a mount saddled up. After I had saluted the General, he said to take a seat. He then asked me if I had received an invitation to have tea at his quarters on Sunday afternoon to which I answered yes, sir. He then said, "But you did not appear." I told him I was in New York on Sunday afternoon. He said, "You did not appear at my tea."

I repeated, "No, sir, I was in New York."

He then said, "Mr. Craig, I don't think you understand, so I am going to explain certain matters to you. You are new to the Service and probably uninformed, but whenever you receive an invitation from a General Officer, and especially when that General Officer is your commander, that invitation takes precedence over everything else. It is the same as an order and it is one of the very oldest customs of the service. Do you understand now?"

I was petrified at this stern old man lecturing to me. I finally squeaked out a "Yes, sir" and he said that would be all and dismissed me. So our Air Service score, between Hill and me, was not too good. The following Friday, I received another invitation to tea, which I attended punctually. It was actually a delightful affair, the host and hostess charming. Everyone there, especially the ladies, wanted to know what an aviator was doing with the 1st Division. The General's lecture stood me in good stead in the years to come.

A week before Christmas, I received orders to proceed to Carlstrom Field, Florida, for a course in pilot training. Hill, who already had a pilot rating, was ordered to Bolling Field, Washington, D.C. This was a serious mistake. He should have been sent to Carlstrom for a refresher course in flying. I do not believe that he did much flying in France and none at all for about two years after leaving the Army. In the months following, I heard he had been in a serious crash at Bolling, and I believe he was retired for some disability shortly afterward.

At Taylor Field, Alabama in 1919

X

1921: Carlstrom Field, A Jenny Incident

AT CARLSTROM I had exceptional luck in being assigned to a flight with three instructors who were probably among the very best pilots in the service: Hez McClelan (his first name must have been Hezekiah), who later became a test pilot at Mc-Cook Field; Fred I. Patrick, a tall, slim man with an aquiline face — I later served with him in Hawaii; and Johnny Corkille, also a test pilot at McCook Field and during World War Two, stationed in Equatorial Africa where he died. Johnny had been stationed with me at Taylor Field in 1919 and knew the thoroughness of the course of instruction given there.

Charles C. Chauncey was in charge of the ground instruction at Carlstrom; Chris Ford, who had served with the French Lafayette Escadrille and an American squadron in France in the First War, was in charge of flying; and Major Ralph Royce was the Commanding Officer.

Some of the other students in this class were Lt. Col. Charles Danforth, a Spanish-American War veteran who had served in the Air Service in a non-flying capacity during World War I; Francis P. "Pat" Booker, a bombardier after his pilot rating; Walter T. Meyer, an RMA taking the refresher course who had served in Italy in World War I; M. G. Estabrook, an engineering officer taking the RMA course; Henry F. Sessions, a pilot also taking the refresher; and a wild man named Oscar Barney, who later transferred out of the Air Service.

I made my first solo at Carlstrom after one hour and forty minutes dual instruction. From then on, most of my air time was solo, with a check ride by one of the instructors about once a week. I remember one incident that happened while I was stationed at Carlstrom, which caused considerable amusement among the mechanics. I was scheduled to make a cross-country flight to Tampa and return, and the morning of the flight turned out to be overcast with a ceiling of about 1000 feet, clouds thin to occasionally broken. I laid out my compass course on the map and with no weather reports to guide me, I estimated the wind to be from the west at about five miles per hour — a head wind going to Tampa. I estimated my ground speed and the time I should reach my destination, then took off in a JN4-D and went up through the thin overcast, losing all sight of land. After flying the time I figured would be required to put me over Tampa, about one hour, I came down through the overcast and found myself out over the Gulf of Mexico with the shore line barely visible behind me. I turned around and finally reached the shore, but after miscalculating my time so badly I could not determine if Tampa lay to the north or south of my position. Picking up some smoke on the ground, I noticed that it was blowing from the north and much stronger than the five miles per hour I had estimated. Anyway, I decided I was south of Tampa and started to fly north. I could identify nothing on the ground with my Rand-McNally road and railroad map. I flew along, still doubtful that I could have drifted so far off my plotted course, and decided to land to get my bearings. I saw a long, narrow pasture running north and south which looked good, and after "dragging" it a few times (flying low to spot obstacles to landing), I went in. I drifted to the right as I came in, and just after touching down, my right wing hit a fence post, tearing the doped linen fabric. I shut the engine off immediately. Fortunately, the impact had not been enough to swing the nose of the plane around into the fence or I would have been in serious trouble. I got out of the plane and inspected the wing. The metal form which shaped the wing's tip was bent a little but I was able to straighten it with my hands. But if I flew the plane with the linen torn loose, the wing might shed all its fabric.

About this time a farmer drove up in a Model-T Ford and asked me if I needed any help. I said said, "Yes, I do. First, I would like to know where Tampa is." He pointed north up the coast and said it lay about thirty miles distant. I could not understand why I had not seen it from the air because the visibility was good. I told the farmer I would have to find a store where I could buy a pillow slip, some shellac and a brush. When we returned, I fitted the pillow slip over the wing tip and then painted it on, using nearly a gallon of shellac. While we were waiting for the shellac to dry, I asked my man to help me move the plane away from the fence so I could taxi to a flat place for takeoff. After an hour, I started the engine, taxied back to the south end of the pasture and took off. It required thirty minutes for me to make the thirty miles to Tampa, where, after fueling and looking over my repair job, I took off again to return to Carlstrom. No more above-the-clouds flying for me.

Hez McClelan met me at the field and asked why I was so late. I had to tell him what had happened and he went over to look at my repair job, calling the crew chief and the Engineering Officer to come and see. The Engineering Officer said it was a good job but he did not know how they would ever get the pillow case off the wing, for it was cemented on solid. They kept the airplane on exhibition for several days to show everyone how field repairs were made. I never knew if they were ridiculing or praising my handiwork.

At Kelly Field, Texas in 1921

XI

1921: Ferrying DH's — Kelly Field, McAllen, Marfa

IN MARCH, 1921, I was ordered to Kelly Field, San Antonio, Texas, and assigned to the 11th Squadron of the Ist Day Bombardment Group (later designated the 2nd Bombardment Group). The Commanding Officer of the 11th Squadron was 1st Lt. Edward Raley. This squadron had its full complement of airplanes (12 DH-4s — DeHaviland's, a British type which we had gotten the license to build; a biplane with a 300-HP engine, two-seater, and nice to fly). With Raley the only officer, he assigned me, the only *other* officer, to be in charge of operations and engineering, supply, and the mess.

Our Group Operations Officer at that time was Lieutenant William J. McKierman, he who had checked me out on the DH-4. The Group Commander, Major John N. Reynolds, had a fine record as an observation group commander overseas.

About the time I had logged ten or fifteen solo hours on the DH-4, a number of trainees arrived at Kelly. Raley required me to fly every airplane we had in commission each day before turning them over to the students. In addition to this, we had to fly the trainees on their camera obscura (bombing training) and their practice runs with actual bombs.

In June we were ordered to ferry back all the airplanes that had been used in the Border Air Patrol. Airplanes were located at such Texas border towns as McAllen, Laredo, Del Rio, Sanderson and Marfa. I remember an incident that occurred at McAllen, where there were five or six DH's to be ferried back. This meant that twelve pilots were engaged in the undertaking, six to fly down the other six ferry pilots, all returning to Kelly solo.

Major Blackburn Hall, a student pilot, was placed in charge of us. He had to bring back to Kelly a sample of gasoline from each of the storage tanks for analysis. He was able to find regular gas cans for all except the last tank, and for this he used a quart tequila bottle, after washing it out carefully. He brought this sample up to his room in the hotel in McAllen. This hotel had a large open space over the lobby leading up to a skylight in the roof. A balcony ran around the second floor and the rooms opened onto this balcony. Three or four of us were sitting in Major Hall's room, waiting for him to get cleaned up for dinner, when the door burst open and a big fellow in western clothes, gun in his hand, entered. He said he was the sheriff of these parts and he was looking for "Tosi" and he knew he was in this room. All the while he waved the revolver around. Hall asked him to put the gun away, saying there was no Tosi here. The "sheriff" was terribly drunk, and I could see no lawman's badge on him. He then holstered his gun and said, "How about a drink?" Hall replied that no liquor was available, and just about that time the fellow's eye landed on the tequila bottle on the floor in a corner. Before anyone could stop him, he sprang over to the bottle, pulled the cork and took a big slug — at least two fingers. He practically exploded — coughing and snorting, with tears streaming down his face — and once again the gun was in his hand. He wanted to know which s.o.b. had done this to him. One of the boys had been edging toward the door while all this was going on, and when the fellow had taken his drink of gasoline, our pilot opened the door and fled down the balcony to the stairway. The drunk saw him out of the corner of his eye and shouted, "There goes Tosi!" dashed to the door and fired a couple of shots down the balcony. The real sheriff, who happened to be in the lobby, raced up to our room where the drunk was still spitting and coughing up gasoline. The sheriff promptly relieved him of his revolver and took him downstairs under arrest. Major Hall had to replenish his tequila bottle of gasoline the next day.

The airplanes we were to ferry back to Kelly were in frightful shape. They had been wheeled into the McAllen hangar and left there with no maintenance for nearly two years. Tires were flat, and the radiators were stuffed with dauber's nests. I learned later that several of the planes had stood for days in an open field during the Corpus Christi flood in 1919. It required a full day to get them cleaned up, with the engines running smoothly. As each pilot became satisfied with the condition of his plane, he would take off for Kelly. I suspect I had the worst of the lot, for I was the last one out of McAllen. Soon after take-off I found that my DH was very tail heavy, even with the stabilizer rolled all the way forward. This required me to push forward on the stick all the way back to Kelly, where I had to think about the kind of landing I would make. It was pitch dark by the time I reached Kelly so I circled around over the field a couple of times, testing various landing approaches — engine half on, all the way off. I found that when I cut the throttle all the way back, the nose would fall with a little help from the stick, so I started my approach for my first night landing. By coming in at half throttle, I could establish a fairly satisfactory glide. A critical factor was that the plane responded very sensitively to a backward pull on the stick, so I had to be very light-handed as I approached the ground. With the help of the throttle I got down without trouble, other than landing faster than normal. I found out later that the DH had to be completely re-rigged, something I could not undertake at McAllen. All the planes we ferried back to Kelly had to go to the Depot for overhaul.

In the latter part of the same month, I was awakened very early one morning by an orderly who told me I was scheduled to leave in an hour or so for Marfa, to ferry back a plane left in the hangar there by the Border Air Patrol when it was closed out early in 1920. I would be flown to Marfa by Lieutenant Jack Glasscock, a superb pilot and flying instructor, a teetotaling bachelor who smoked the rankest pipe that ever existed. I heard that he had been an excellent athlete, but at this time he had gotten bald, homely and fat, with a regular Santa Claus belly. He also had a terrible time with his clothes — uniforms never seemed to fit him properly, and while he had a fancy for yellow boots, even they seemed sloppy. But whatever the case for his appearance, he was a very fine, unselfish person, well liked by his fellow officers.

He was waiting for me when I got out to the line, and said we would be back that same evening so there was no use taking any baggage. We wore khaki breeches, boots, and a wool O.D. shirt with tie. We soon got away and, with good weather, landed at Marfa about 10:30 a.m.

We opened the hangar doors and rolled the DH out in the sunlight. It appeared to be in pretty good shape, except for the eternal water dauber nests in the radiator cores. Jack and I worked the rest of the morning clearing out the nests and then phoned to the transportation section for a ride to the Officer's Club. Even after cleaning up we looked a mess. After lunch, we got a spring wagon to take us back to the hangar, and after servicing both planes from 50 gallon drums, we were ready to take off. Jack swung my prop through, the engine catching on the first try — an oddity. Blocking the wheels and leaving my DH to idle, I swung Jack's prop, which also caught on the first try. While I was warming and revving up the engine, a uniformed horseman appeared at a gallop. (As I look back on it, here was a strange mingling of eras — horseman and aviator.) He pulled up alongside my plane and asked me to identify myself. I explained about ferrying the plane back to Kelly, and he asked to see my orders. Neither Jack Glasscock nor I had written orders; everything had been verbal. The horseman said he was the Officer of the Day for the cavalry post and that the post had been given custody of the hangar and its contents, including the DH — which I could not take away without written orders. I said, "Suppose I just open the throttle and take off. . . . What would happen?" When he guessed that he would probably end up in the guardhouse, I cut the engine off and asked him to send a priority message to the CO of Kelly Field. He galloped off toward his headquarters. In the meantime Jack had grown impatient with the delay and taxied his plane over near mine. He was very unhappy when I explained the situation, and offered to stay with me to resolve the problem. We pushed the two airplanes back in the hangar, locked it, and phoned for some transportation to the BOQ. This time the transportation people sent down a Daugherty wagon drawn by two mules. It seemed to me that our stock was going down — or maybe it was going up as a Daugherty wagon (a four-wheel, two-horse affair, and very sturdy) was considered among the best in wagon transportation.

Fortunately, the mess at the Officer's Club accepted our chits so at least we could eat. After a bath and shave we had to put the same old clothes on, and I resolved to wash out my underwear and socks before we went to bed. They were getting ripe after our labors with the water daubers.

At the mess that night, Jack and I felt like a couple of bums. Our grease-streaked breeches and shirts and our dirty boots compared poorly with the spit-and-polish of the cavalry officers. We took a table near the door and ate in silence, feeling a little sorry for ourselves. We were of much interest to the cavalry garrison, and this was the first time I felt the hostility of the ground officer for the aviator. It was very real; no one spoke to us. Even the Officer of the Day, the captain who prevented our takeoff, ignored us.

Down to my last dollar the next morning, I got a mount from one of the troops and made my way into town, found a pawn shop and borrowed $10 on the closed faced pocket watch which my mother had given me on my 18th birthday.

When I returned, Jack and I went down to the QM clothing store for a couple of campaign hats, clean breeches and cotton shirts. We felt much more reputable after that. Jack, with his fair skin and bald noggin, had particular need of a hat whenever he went out in the midsummer sun of west Texas.

We were in Marfa three days. Finally the Adjutant came over to us while we were eating breakfast and said that confirming orders had come in during the night and we could leave any time we were ready. I have never believed any message was sent to Kelly Field as I had requested, and that the old curmudgeon of a Colonel of the Fifth Cavalry had decided to give us young upstarts a lesson.

We got a ride to the hangar, wheeled both planes out, and took off. Both of us were glad to get out of Marfa.

Upon our return, I reported our experiences to Major Reynolds, but I never learned if he reported our treatment to higher headquarters. Jack and I settled up our debt with the Fifth Cavalry mess office by sending them a check, and I sent the Marfa pawnbroker the money to redeem my watch.

XII

1921-23: *Evangeline, Langley Field, Martin Bombers*

THE SUMMER PASSED without unusual incident — ex-
✻   cept that during this time I met my future wife, Evangeline
Bateman, at a Saturday night dance at Kelly's Officer's Club.
She and I were to have been blind dates, but I chickened out and went
to the dance stag. She too had gone solo and we were, somewhat em-
barrassingly, thrown together with me apologizing and spluttering. After that dance we were together whenever I could get away from the
job and I married this wonderful young lady on September 1, 1921.

In the middle of June, 1922, orders arrived from Washington, directing the 2nd Bombardment Group and its four squadrons to move
by troop train to Langley Field, Virginia — the move to be completed
by June 30. The doctors would not permit Evangeline to travel by
train, so she and her parents, Chaplain and Mrs. Cephas Bateman, followed me after our baby Jeanne was born early that August. The Bate-
mans visited for a month.

We arrived at Langley early in the afternoon of June 30 to meet the
Commanding Officer, Lt. Col. Charles H. Danforth (who had proceeded to Langley when he completed his flying training at Kelly in June),
his Executive Officer, Major H. G. Clagett, and the Adjutant, Captain
L. P. Jacobs, who had prepared the assignment of quarters and barracks.

Langley was a permanent base built during World War I for the
National Advisory Committee on Aeronautics but turned over to the
War Department. It is located near Hampton, Virginia.

Because my family had not yet joined me, I had quarters in the light-
er-than-air section of the post, a most undesirable billet because of the
distance I would have to travel to my work. However, when I received

word of Evangeline's imminent arrival, I was given very satisfactory quarters on the regular post. By this time, with the baby, we were settling into family life, as much as the military can "settle."

I had the assignment of Operations Officer, Adjutant and Commanding Officer of Headquarters Squadron, 2nd Bombardment Group. As the only officer so assigned, these three jobs kept me more than busy. We began our transition to the Martin Bomber forthwith. At the beginning only two or three of these airplanes were available. Capt. Walter "Shorty" Lawson became commander of the 20th Squadron, placed in charge of the transition flying. Major Blackburn Hall was designated Group Commander; Capt. Edward C. Black was Commander of the 96th Squadron; 1st Lt. Aubrey Hornsby commanded the 11th Squadron; and 1st Lt. William Hayward, the 59th Service Squadron.

I had considerable trouble with the MBs, particularly on turns. Either I would give the machine too much rudder or not enough. My instructors were a Lt. Ray Davis and another "Shorty," Lt. C. M. Cummings. Cummings thought I was too tense, Davis thought I was too relaxed. I did better with Shorty Cummings but Capt. Lawson did not like my effort at all. He was a very strict individual, lacking all sense of humor and very intolerant of what he judged to be incompetence. He had been an artillery observer in France and learned to fly pretty much on his own after the Armistice.

After we had been at Langley about a month, Major Hall was discharged from the service and we received Major John N. Reynolds as our Group Commander. He was a fine commander and had a distinguished record overseas during the war.

About this time we were allotted the entire production of the new Martin Bomber being manufactured by Curtiss at Mineola on Long Island and Aeromarine at Keyport, New Jersey. The airplane had the designation NBSI (Night Bomber, Short Distance, 1st model) and was quite similar to the MB2 (Martin Medium Bomber, 2nd model). It had a few improvements over the older machine but not many. One change involved alteration of a rawhide pinion which would mesh with a steel gear on the fuel pump of the engines. After about two hours, the rawhide gear would wear out, causing a stoppage of the engine.

We were detailed by roster to ferry the airplanes from the factory on Long Island and at Keyport to Langley and soon each squadron had charge of nine airplanes.

During this period we learned that we were to bomb the battleships *Virginia* and *New Jersey* during the summer, and intensive training in bombing and night flying was started. About this time, Captain Lawson died in an airplane crash at McCook Field, Dayton, Ohio, and Captain Lloyd L. Harvey was transferred into the Group to take the 20th Squadron. The complete opposite of Lawson, Captain Harvey was a small man, quiet, gentle, very considerate and a superb pilot. It became my good fortune to be teamed up with him as his bombardier.

The bombing of the battleships was scheduled for the summer of 1923. In the spring of that year, Major Reynolds was relieved of command of the Group, and Captain Harvey took over. Captain E. E. W. Duncan assumed command of the 59th Service Squadron and Lieutenant Gresham of the 20th Squadron.

XIII

1922-23: *Airways Flight, "Sue" Clagett*

❂ IN THE LATTER PART OF 1922, it came my turn to make the "Airways Flight." General William "Billy" Mitchell, the Assistant Chief of the Air Service, had established an eastern and western model airway and made it a rule that every pilot would fly the air route in his part of the country at least once. The eastern airway extended from Mitchel and Langley Fields to Washington, thence to Moundsville, West Virginia, and on to Dayton, Ohio. Under a later expansion, it included Chanute Field in Illinois, and Scott Field, east of St. Louis. I got off in a DH4 in the early morning of a beautiful, clear day, made a stop for gas at Moundsville and arrived at Dayton (McCook Field) that evening without difficulty.

At McCook, crewmen installed an instrument on the dashboard of my airplane called a "bank and turn indicator." When I asked the mechanic how it worked, he said it was simple: "just keep the pointer and the ball together." The ball floated in the instrument something like the bubble in a carpenter's spirit level.

On the return flight and stopover at Moundsville, the weather looked good. Proper weather forecasting formed a big handicap in aviation in those days, for the Weather Bureau, then a part of the Department of Agriculture, issued its reports and forecasts with an orientation toward farming. This situation lasted for many years until the Bureau was removed from the USDA and made an independent agency.

After servicing the DH at Moundsville, I collected a passenger, climbed aboard and took off. Soon we were about 7,000 feet over the Allegheny Mountains, passing through one cloud puff after another. We entered a large cloud formation, and after several minutes I decided we had better get a little more altitude. (This was my first experience in blind flying.) I eased back on the stick and I happened to glance down at my newly installed bank-and-turn indicator to discover the pointer in one corner and the ball in the other. I then looked at my airspeed indicator and saw it resting on 60 m.p.h. We were in a slow spin, and I immediately pushed the stick forward, centering it and the rudder. The airspeed came back up to 90 and the pointer and ball of the bank-and-turn indicator were more or less centered. My altitude was still around 7,000 feet, but when I looked at my compass, I found my heading north instead of east. I made a gradual flat turn and headed back east, but the point that bothered me was how far off course to the north I had flown. I edged the plane more toward the southeast, and in a few minutes broke out of the clouds, just about over Winchester, Virginia. In the now clear sunshine I headed south and soon picked up Front Royal, Virginia, on the good old Rand-McNally road map. I nosed the plane over slightly to lose altitude, and when nearly over the Naval Radio Towers at Arlington with about 500 feet altitude, the engine suddenly conked out. Although the wind came from the north, it was very light, and I decided to go straight into Bolling Air Field, Washington, D.C., the trick being to maintain the precise airspeed to land across the narrow part of the field. As soon as I reached the edge of the field I made a short side slip and then "fishtailed" with the rudder until we landed. The plane rolled and rolled, finally winding up in the space between the hangars. My passenger climbed out and said he had a nice ride and thanked me. I am sure, to this day, he had no idea of the trouble we had been in just minutes before.

I explained to the line chief what had happened over the radio towers, and the first thing he looked at was the oil level. The dipstick showed empty. The engine had not frozen, and after filling it with a light oil, it seemed to run perfectly.

The next morning, I left for Langley, landing there a little over an hour later. Much to my surprise, quite a delegation had gathered to meet me. Later I found out that the four pilots who had preceded me on the roster had cracked up at different places enroute, and the fact that I had the luck to complete the flight safely restored the reputation of the field.

DURING THE WINTER of 1922-23, orders were received at Langley to initiate a program of "formal guard mount." Major Henry Clagett, a West Pointer (class of '08) and very strict but with the gentle nickname of "Sue," was placed in charge of this project and he decided the initial step, after getting a band organized, should be sabre drill by all officers. First of all, we had to buy sabres, then we practiced until the Major decided we were reasonably safe and competent.

Being adjutant of the Group, I was designated to conduct the guard mount exercise. A new regulation had recently been published concerning formal guard mount which changed the old method to some extent. On the first day of the exercise, for some reason unknown to me the ceremonies were scheduled for two o'clock in the afternoon. The entire population of the post turned out to witness the great event that bright and warm spring day. With the band playing merrily, I lined up the old and new guards, gave the pass in review orders, and the troops began the march to their respective destinations. Suddenly, I heard someone shouting, "Mr. Craig, Mr. Craig! Halt your detachments and come here!" Sue Clagett had gotten into the act. When I reported to him, he said, "You are doing a part of this wrong. Do it over again." For the life of me, I could not imagine what was wrong; nevertheless, I arranged the old and new sections of the guard and started over again. Again, the shout of "Mr. Craig!" flew across the parade ground. The spectators were enjoying the show immensely. This time I asked Major Clagett to be specific about what I was doing wrong. He replied, "If you knew your drill regulations, you would know what you are doing wrong. However, I will explain your mistake to you." When he finished, I told him the part of the regulation he referred to had been changed. To prove it, I hauled out the new little manual of Interior Guard Duty from my hip pocket and started to leaf through it to find the changed paragraphs. When I looked up, the Major had departed. I saw Col. Danforth and Captain Jacobs standing nearby, roaring with laughter. Afterward, I found out that I had committed the unforgivable sin of "pulling the book" on my superior officer.

Sue Clagett, a shrewd man, did not allow me to get away with the book episode. The next day I received an order, signed by Major Clagett, Executive Officer, detailing me to act as Adjutant for the formal guard mount until further notice and, in addition, to give calisthenics to all the troops of the post each morning, weather permitting, following reveille formation. This meant daily except Sunday, until relieved by order, and this old devil came out to make sure I was doing my job.

One day at the end of the month I had gone through my routine and had given the order for the 1st sergeants to dismiss the troops, when I heard the 1st Sergeant of my Group Headquarters Squadron reading out work details for the day. While listening, I unconsciously filled my pipe, intending to remind the 1st Sergeant that this being pay day, he should not assign any payroll clerks to fatigue details. After getting this over with, I started to walk away from the formation, stopping momentarily to light my pipe, when out from behind a hangar stepped Major Clagett, calling, "Mr. Craig! Mr. Craig!" I walked over to him, saluted and waited. He snapped, "Mr. Craig, you know better, certainly, than to smoke a pipe while in formation with your troops!"

I said, "Yes sir, but I was not in formation with the troops. I had already dismissed them and was only waiting until the 1st Sergeant had finished reading his fatigue details for the day."

"I consider," he retorted, "that you were in the presence of your troop while they were in formation and you should not have been smoking," to which I replied with the standard "Yes, sir."

He proceeded, "Besides, I do not understand how you can smoke a pipe before breakfast." (*He* was also a pipe smoker.) I told him I already *had* breakfast, and he exclaimed, "My God, man, how can you go through with all those calisthenics on a full stomach?"

I answered, "I never would be able to give those vigorous exercises without having something to eat."

Whereupon he asked, "Where did you have breakfast?" "The 96th Squadron and a very good one," I offered. He said, "Let's go over and give it another try." *We* did and with much congratulating of the cook and KP's.

XIV

1923: Billy Mitchell, Bombing the Virginia and New Jersey

⊛ AS SPRING WORE ON TO SUMMER, we worked harder at our formation and night flying, taking more and more bombing practice with 100 pound bombs. Since all of us were rated pilots, as group operations officer I had to select some pilots and designate them as bombardiers. I tried to match men with the most flying experience with men with the least. I drew up individual training programs in each squadron for each month, showing the amount of bombing practice required, formation and night flying, together with charts showing what had been accomplished to date.

As the time for the bombing of the battleships approached, General Billy Mitchell visited us more frequently. He was a youngish-looking man — imperially slim, erect and well dressed. He had a knack as a good listener and a shrewd interrogator who made no apology for "picking another man's brains." An articulate man, he had great vision and imagination, but he was not so much loved as *admired*. Egocentric to the degree he would not accept advice, he accomplished much for American aviation, but could have accomplished more.

One morning after calisthenics I went to my office and found my operations sergeant already there. I began some paperwork, when General Mitchell walked in the door. He asked me if I always got down to the office so early. I explained the calisthenics affair to him and said that it was just as easy to start work after the exercises as later. I showed him my charts of what we had accomplished in flying and bombing practice in the Group and what we proposed to do further. He thought we had a fine system and expressed the view that all our tactical units should be doing the same thing. (In fact, within a year an order came out in an attempt to start such a scheme.) At this same time we had begun to keep maintenance charts on our aircraft. These charts would show when inspections should be made of the various parts of the airplanes and engines, trouble reported by pilots, aircraft out of commission and why. I accompanied General Mitchell on this particular morning to the 96th Squadron Hangar, and we went over the maintenance charts with the hangar NCO.

On one of these unannounced early morning visits, General Mitchell, accompanied by his aide Lieutenant Clayton Bissell in another airplane, and in still another Colonel James Fechet, stormed into the Group Operations office and instructed me to assemble all the officers of the Group in front of the hangar. In about fifteen minutes he and his party arrived and the General outlined a tactical problem much like the following: "The enemy is attempting to land a force at Cape Hatteras. It consists of three transports supported by two battleships, three cruisers and a number of destroyers. The 2nd Bombardment Group will attack this force, destroying the transports and the supporting forces. The 11th Squadron will load with the maximum number of 300 pound demolition bombs and attack the transports.

"The 20th Squadron will load with the maximum number of 600 pound and 1000 pound demolition bombs and attack the cruisers.

"The 96th Squadron will load a 2000 pound bomb on each airplane and attack the battleships.

"Captain Harvey will command the Group."

He then instructed me to prepare a Field Order for the operation. At that time I had never heard of a Field Order, but Colonel Fechet caught up with me on my dash to the office and we prepared a draft of the order. Olsen, the operations sergeant, knocked out enough copies for each squadron Commander, and these were delivered before they took off for the exercise. General Mitchell took a hasty glance at his copy, gave me a hard look, and stuffed the paper in his pocket.

Finally, the day for the bombing exercise arrived September 5. We all flew down to Cape Hatteras in the early morning of a beautiful, clear day, and landed on the beach at low tide. Our Service Squadron had worked all night unloading bombs, gasoline, oil and other supplies, and delivering them to the Squadrons. Very few of us had ever seen a 2000 pound bomb, and certainly none of us had ever dropped one. Captain Harvey, in a 96th Squadron plane with me as his bombardier, supervised the loading of the 2000-pounder on our Martin during the morning. It would not be armed until time for take-off. After a frugal lunch we all went back to our airplanes. We were scheduled to be the first off, and as we were taxiing toward the take-off point, I noticed that the fins of our bomb were dragging in the sand. The armed bomb was a cause of considerable concern. When I told the Captain about it, he decided to get out and take a look. Our Ordnance Officer, Captain Stribling, came up on the run and looked the situation over, finally giving his okay for take-off. We taxied down to the hard-packed sand left by the outgoing tide and took off without any difficulty. The other planes formed up behind us in a single file and we headed out to sea. The two battleships, *Virginia* and *New Jersey* were barely visible, and Captain Harvey on approaching them lined us up fore and aft of the ships which were almost into the wind. Both ships were under way although it seemed to me they were moving very slowly. I pointed to the leading battleship, the *Virginia*, as the one I wanted and Captain Harvey made a small adjustment in his course to accommodate me. I made some allowance for the speed of the old battlewagon as we approached it, and when the cross hairs were amidships, I pulled the release lever — and nothing happened. I then gave it a tremendous yank and the bomb fell away. But the brief hesitation caused me to overshoot and the bomb landed about fifty yards off the bow of the ship. We immediately banked to the left just in time to see the second bomber score his shot in the water, immediately amidships. The force was such that the battleship almost turned over on her side. The third and fourth planes did some good marksmanship on the other target ship with the 2,000 pound bomb. The planes with the lighter bombs followed and finished off the *Virginia* and *New Jersey* sending them to the bottom of the sea.

The Group quickly reformed in a V formation and started back to the base at Langley. Needless to say, we were all very much elated by the performance and when General Mitchell arrived he congratulated

us profusely. He announced an officers meeting the next morning at
ten o'clock in Headquarters Building, where he again congratulated all
of us for a very fine performance and then went on to predict the future
of the bomber airplane, saying at the end that the range, speed and
altitude of future planes would exceed our wildest imagination.

In full flying gear in 1929

XV

1923: Night Flying

✦ IN SEPTEMBER, 1923, we received a new Group Commander in Major John Pirie, a Coast Artillery man who had completed the flying school course and won his wings. In his latter forties he had accomplished a considerable feat at such an age, in completing the flying schools. He was a pleasant, soft-spoken man, very anxious to learn all about this new branch of the service.

He soon started us on a new and thorough program of night flying. In fact, although we had been doing some night flying, for a time under his command we flew more at night than in the daytime, and at that time, there was very little night flying done in the Air Corps. Facilities for flying at night were nonexistent. A Lieutenant Donald Bruner at McCook Field tried to develop lights for landing, spending much time with our Group. These landing lights were placed near the wing tips, but they had a serious defect: they would burn out about one minute after being turned on. We also carried wing tip and parachute flares. The latter type was developed to illuminate a large area in order to pick out a place to land. This system involved flying over the possible landing place into the wind at about 1000 feet altitude, dropping the parachute flare and immediately starting 360-degree turn, losing altitude, and when close to the ground, igniting the wing tip flares for landing. It was a fairly good system.

Bruner was also interested in obstacle lighting. Around the flying field the big question revolved around putting red obstacle lights on all the structures that might interfere with a landing or illuminating them with flood lights. This was like choosing between vanilla and chocolate: Some people favored one, some the other. I believe the final decision favored the use of red obstacle lights.

In October, Major Pirie decided we had enough night flying training and scheduled a night flight for the whole group from Langley to Mitchel. We were all flying NBS-1's and I was teamed with Capt. Willis Hale as navigator. Also in the plane was Capt. Harold L. Mc-Clellan who was experimenting with a radio set. When we were over Lakehurst, New Jersey (where, in 1937, the zeppelin *Hindenberg* burned while mooring), Capt. Hale suddenly became sick and vomited all over the cockpit.

Hale asked me to take over the controls and we had an awful time exchanging seats because these bombers had only one set of controls, and we had our parachutes on in a clumsy arrangement. I brought the plane into Mitchel with no additional trouble, however, and only one plane in our flight had to land at Lakehurst. As that field's floodlamps burned out as he approached the runway, he had to use his wing-tip flares.

XVI

1923: Rhode Island Mishap

ON ONE OF GENERAL MITCHELL'S TRIPS a few weeks later, he announced the Group would undertake a field exercise to Old Orchard Beach, Maine, to determine how long we could live and function on the materials and equipment we carried with us.

For this exercise, the Group had to be divided into an advance echelon, a main body, and a support force. I was designated to be in the advance echelon, together with Capt. Early W. Duncan, the Service Squadron Commander, and Lt. "Shorty" Cummings. In the teeth of a strong north wind, we three took off one morning, each plane loaded to the gills. Five hours later we landed at Mitchel Field, New York, and decided to call it a day.

The wind died down during the night, and we were off in NBS1s early the next morning for Old Orchard. While flying along in a loose V-formation over Rhode Island, I noticed the temperature on the right engine had risen to near boiling. The crew chief pointed out that the shutters were closed but the little lever that regulated them showed open. These manual, thermo-controlled shutters controlled the flow of impact air for radiator cooling. The coiled spring that held the shutters open had broken, permitting them to close. I idled the engine, and we gradually lost altitude. Boston was the next airport, but I did not believe we could make it, even if I occasionally used the hot engine. The crew chief wanted to crawl out on the wing and rip the shutters out with his hands, but this would have been so hazardous, I forbade him, and started to look the country over for a place to make an emergency landing. Finally I spotted a race track which seemed to offer possibilities and landed, stopping within ten feet of a deep old gravel pit completely overgrown with grass and shrubs. I shut down the engines, and the crew chief repaired the shutter spring in a few minutes. But a crowd gathered about the plane, and the one Massachusetts State policeman who appeared could not keep them back. I did not dare to start the engines, fearing someone would walk into the propellers. The policeman told me he would phone for help but when he returned he said his boss would not send any more men because we were in Rhode Island, and he would have to phone the Rhode Island police to help us. In the meantime the crowd increased by the minute, with children trying to puncture the linen on the wings or obtain some kind of souvenir. Presently the Rhode Island police arrived and maneuvered the crowd behind the railings of the track. I started the engines and taxied to the takeoff point, but as there was absolutely no wind, I had very serious doubts about getting the plane off and clearing the trees on the far end with the heavy load I had aboard. I finally decided to lay over until the next day.

My crew chief suggested that we unload most of our cargo such as the field range, cans of food, record files, typewriters, and flags (being Headquarters Squadron) and ship it all up to Old Orchard by railway express. This suggestion struck me as a good idea and we began unloading the airplane.

While we were thus engaged, a good-looking man approached me, introduced himself, said he had served in the submarines during the war and asked me if he could be of any help. I told him I had two immediate problems: to find transportation to haul all our baggage to the Express Office and, to find a place where two enlisted men and I could stay for the night. He said he had some trucks which he could make available for the first problem, and as to the second, there was a boarding house down the road about a quarter of a mile, run by a French-Canadian woman. He thought it would be satisfactory for the men, and as for me, he would be happy to share his apartment with me for the night but I would have to look after my meals. He ate, he said, in a little cafeteria near where he lived. I thanked him for his offer and accepted. I told him I did not have much money to pay for his trucks, but he said that would be all right.

After getting the two trucks loaded and verifying the police guard for the plane over night, we climbed aboard the vehicles and headed for town. On the way we stopped at the boarding house and the woman said she could take the two men, give them supper and breakfast the next morning and pack a lunch for them for one dollar each. I paid her the two dollars and made arrangements for them to get out to the race track early the next morning. We then went downtown to the Pawtucket Express office, where, with the help of the truck drivers and the Express man, we unloaded the trucks and sent the baggage on its way. I gave the Express man a Government Bill of Lading for the shipment which was addressed to "General William Mitchell, Old Orchard Beach, Maine." (I learned afterward that it arrived in time to be of use.) My submariner friend picked me up and drove me to his apartment in mid-town. On the way he explained that he was in the trucking and hauling business. After a bath, we went out to his cafeteria and had supper. I went back to the apartment after eating, and he off somewhere. In a short time, I crawled into bed — I had had a busy day.

We were up early the next morning and after breakfast, my civilian drove me out to the race track where my crew awaited. The crew chief had gone over the motors and warmed them up, but still there was no wind. The weather bureau in Pawtucket proved no help in determining possible wind conditions later in the day and so I decided to take off. I paced off the distance between my plane and the far side of the race track — approximately 2,000 feet. Because I would have to clear the trees on the far side of the track, I finally estimated I would use about 1200 - 1500 feet before leaving the ground. We put blocks under the wheels and started the engines. I ran both the engines up to maximum RPM before the plane jumped the blocks. Gathering speed very quickly, we were off the ground at a little over 1000 feet. However, in passing over the inside rail fence of the track, the wheels touched the fence for a split second, just enough to cause the nose of the plane to dip. Seeing I would hit the tops of some of the taller trees, I eased back on the controls — but not soon enough.

We struck the taller tree tops and then plunged into the others. I immediately cut both switches and turned off the gasoline to the en-

gines — again too late, and one of the engines caught fire. The crew
chief got out a hand-held fire extinguisher and soon had the blaze controlled.

So there we were, parked in the trees about ten feet off the ground.
My first concern was for the man in the back cockpit. He did not answer our calls, and I crawled back to find him stunned from a crack
on the head. My sergeant crew chief scrambled down while I worked
on the sergeant major in the rear cockpit, who finally came to and in
a few minutes was able to lower himself to the ground. I followed
them down.

A crowd of people poured over the race track toward the scene of
the accident. The police had to send for reinforcements. These people
were trying to get scraps of the plane as souvenirs and finally succeeded
in shaking the plane loose from the tree tops. Presently, additional policemen arrived and were able to contain the crowd.

My good friend the submariner asked what he could do. I told him
that I had to send some telegrams back to Langley asking for instructions, to the chief's office, and to General Mitchell at Old Orchard
Beach.

A reply from the Chief's office (the only one I received) came the
next day. It instructed me to ship the wreck to the Fairfield Air Depot,
send the crew chief to Old Orchard and the sergeant major to the Air
Office in Boston. My orders were to proceed to Mitchel Field and wait
for transportation back to Langley. I faced a financial crisis. I had ten
dollars with me and about twenty in my checking account back at
Hampton, some of which my wife would need. Neither of my noncoms
had a cent. I have often wondered where the people in the Chief's office
thought I would get the money to send my men all around New England and myself to New York.

I had to borrow some money, and started looking over the banks in
Pawtucket. Actually, I should have waited to get some advice from my
ex-Navy friend. However, I came across one small bank, marched in
and asked to see the President. The old gentleman sat behind his desk
and looked me over with no little curiosity. I introduced myself and
told him I had wrecked my airplane and needed some money to feed

and bed my two men and myself. He said he had read about the accident in the morning paper and asked how much money I needed. I told him about one hundred dollars. He finally said that the bank could not lend me any money but he would let me have the one hundred out of his own personal account. I thanked him sincerely and accepted his offer.

That afternoon, I advertised in the local newspaper for bids on the crating and hauling of the wreck and arranged with the railroad to spot a box car and a flat car on a siding near the race track. To my surprise, my submarine friend submitted the low bid and I awarded the job to him. He started the disassembly of the plane almost immediately and as a bonus, I gave him the gasoline and oil remaining in the tanks. We braced and cradled the wings and fuselage on the flat car, anchoring the engines and smaller surfaces in the box car. As they finished the job in two days, I thought it well and expeditiously done.

We paid the boarding house for the men and took them down to Pawtucket where we put Sergeant Major Paul Coble on the bus for Boston and Staff Sergeant Berg on the bus for Providence where he could catch a train for Old Orchard Beach. I stopped by the bank to thank the president again for the loan and promised him I would repay as soon as I got back to Langley. After another night with my friend, I caught a bus for New York and then took the Long Island Railroad to Garden City, the stopping place for Mitchel Field. At Mitchel, I found Captain John Colgan of Langley with an empty seat in the rear of his DH and in a short while returned to Langley.

That afternoon I reported to Colonel Danforth, the Commanding Officer of Langley, and told him my story, including the telegram I had received and the loan from the Pawtucket bank. I told him that I thought the Government should arrange in some way to provide emergency funds for such trips. He agreed with me and said would take the matter up with General Mason M. Patrick, the Chief of Air Service. He left for Washington the next day, and when he returned he said that he had related my story to General Patrick, who promised to do something about it. And he did. About a month later, *per diem* funds were made available for reimbursement of expenses at the rate of $8.00

per day for all ordered flights away from the home station. This helped quite a lot, although it did not provide any money *in advance* — when it would be most desperately needed.

A few days later the Group returned from Old Orchard. At that time we were able to put in a voucher called "commutation of rations and quarters," which would pay us in cash the net value of rations and quarters paid out of pocket, but one had to have a written order to go with it. I finally persuaded the base to issue the order for the three of us and then got in touch with Sergeant Coble and Sergeant Berg to have them turn the money over to me to repay the kindly Pawtucket banker.

General Mitchell then arrived at Langley and at a meeting of all the Group officers he told us he was pleased with the performacne of the Group on the exercise and that it had been perfect except for one accident — which was "due to poor judgment on the part of the pilot." I felt like taking issue with him on this point but realized it would be a futile undertaking. Nevertheless, I felt badly about this crack and he lost much of my admiration and respect for saying it.

XVII

1924: Miami Bombing Run

✪ IN JANUARY, 1924, Captain Willis Hale relieved me — literally as well as practically — as Group Operations Officer.

In March that year, the City of Miami invited the Group to send two bomb teams to compete against the Navy as part of a city celebration. Captain Early Duncan and I were selected from Langley and Lieutenant Harold L. George and Captain Romeyn Hough from the 49th Squadron at Aberdeen.

Early Duncan and I alternated at each station in piloting. I had the misfortune to be at the controls when we left Jacksonville (Camp Johnston) and had just passed over Palm Beach when one engine started sputtering. I immediately turned inland, looking for a place to land. Then the NBS-1 engine quit altogether, and as I increased the other engine to full speed, presently *it* started sputtering. I saw what appeared to be a suitable field dead ahead, west of the railroad tracks, and headed for that. I was losing altitude rapidly and it soon became a question of whether I would make it over the telegraph wires paralleling the railroad. To make matters worse a train appeared on the tracks rapidly closing in on my flight path. When I got near the telegraph lines, I pulled back on the controls and barely cleared the wires, but in doing so I lost most of my airspeed and squashed to the ground from a twenty foot height. On first appearance, it looked as if no damage was done to the plane, but closer examination revealed that nearly every fitting anchoring the flying wires had stretched to the breaking point. Getting off a distance from the plane and taking a critical look at it revealed the wings drooping — the landing wire fittings were gone. Early and I then went over the entire plane and decided that it would have to go to a depot for repair.

Harold George flew over where we had landed and we waved him on. The closest town was Del Ray, and Early got a ride there to send a telegram back to Langley, reporting the accident. Several days later we received a reply which instructed us to ship the plane to Fairfield. Remembering my experience at Pawtucket, I inserted an ad in the Del Ray paper asking for bids to disassemble, pack and crate the plane. In the meantime Early caught a train down to Miami, and when he returned, I had awarded the contract to a company whose men and equipment were already hard at work. We soon had the plane aboard the freight cars and on its way to Fairfield Depot in Ohio. Then Early and I with the crew chief caught a local train to Miami, where we were put up in the hotel with Harold George and his crew.

Since we now had only one airplane and two crews, we concentrated on how we could get two shots at the target, a circle laid out on the field. George's airplane was an MB-1 (with a four-wheel landing gear) and flew quite differently than the MB-2 or the NBS-1 which we had. Harold George did not think either Early or I could fly a straight line with it without considerable practice. We finally decided that Harold and Captain Hough would fly the first crack at the target, then land and load up with bombs. For the next try at the target George and Early would be in the pilot seats with me in the bomber compartment and Captain Hough in the rear. We cleared this arrangement with the officials over a Navy protest. On the first round George and his bombardier did not do so well and the Navy was jubilant. Then I went up with him and scored a bull's eye on the first bomb and near misses on the next two. We were awarded the big silver trophy which sat for many years in a case in the Headquarters Building at Langley.

Anxious to get home I went to see the General Passenger Agent of the railroad and persuaded him to let the crew chief and me have tickets back to Langley. I promised him I would send a transportation request immediately as soon as I arrived. Deciding to trust me, he scheduled us on a Pullman leaving that day.

On the way back, Harold George encountered engine trouble and attempted a landing on the parade ground at Paris Island, South Carolina, the Marine Base. He scattered the plane and its liquid contents to the four winds but fortunately no one was hurt.

During the coming summer I made another model airways trip, this time to Scott Field, Illinois, and return. The only incident on this flight was a ten-day layover at Moundsvile, West Virginia, on the return flight. A Captain "Red" Simonin had been in charge of this station for some time, and he knew the weather over the mountains to the east better than anyone. He had a telephone arrangement with the manager of a hotel at Washington, Pa., from whom he could get a report on the approximate height of the clouds. Washington was one of the highest points on the route, and usually if clear of clouds, the rest of the way would be clear. Washington also had the distinction of being one of the places where Walter Brookins, my first aviator friend, put on an exhibition in October, 1910, before huge crowds.

I placed myself completely in Red's hands. The idle hours, while waiting a clear day, I spent at the State Prison in Moundsville. This was a very interesting experience, and I became fairly well acquainted with the prison officials and some of the prisoners.

Finally, one morning we received an all clear message from Washington and I took off. Actually, I had about a thousand-foot ceiling over the mountains and the rest of the way.

XVIII

1925-27: Luke Field, Hawaii

⊛ IN EARLY DECEMBER, 1924, I received orders transferring me to Hawaii and immediately took the sixty days leave granted me. I put my car on the *Nitro*, a Navy ammunition ship scheduled to sail for Pearl Harbor, and bought train tickets for San Diego where Evangeline's mother, father, sister and brother-in-law were living. Also, my brother-in-law, Lieutenant Colonel Charles W. Winnia (a retired cavalryman) kept himself busy in the real estate business there. At this time General Billy Mitchell was being tried by courts martial, and the San Diego papers gave the proceedings full coverage. A large number of Navy people were stationed in San Diego and General Mitchell had leveled serious charges against the Navy Department. The trial proved to be a topic of lively discussion between Charlie Winnia and me and at times, I am sure he baited me about the future of the air service compared to the cavalry.

After our visit ended, we took the train to San Francisco and stayed at the guest house at Crissy Field to await the sailing of our transport. There were about a half dozen Air Service lieutenants along with us on the transport and as soon as we were at sea, we received orders assigning us exclusively to various housekeeping chores aboard the ship. To pour it on a little bit, the troop commander, a major of Infantry, soon published a schedule of "Officer of the Day duty" during the remainder of the voyage. Our names were prominent. But we all lived through it and arrived in Honolulu on a spectacularly bright and sunny day in February, 1925. A host of old friends met us at the pier, among them "Shorty" Cummings, who served in the 2nd Bomb Group with Harold Clark and me, and Mrs. Harold "Sugar" Clark from our Kelly Field days. They soon had Evangeline, our daughter Jeanne and me settled; we picked up our car at the Navy Base, already serviced with gas and oil. We found a house available close to the beach, on Saratoga Road, across the street from the Ft. de Russey tennis courts and moved in.

I had been assigned to Luke Field, 5th Composite Group, 23rd Bombardment Squadron, commanded by Major Karl Gorman, who later was killed when he had engine trouble and had to land in the surf east of Haleiwa. The squadron was taken over by Lieutenant Grandison Gardiner, among the finest men I would ever come to know. After about a month in Hawaii, I had to tow a target at night for the Anti-Aircraft Artillery at Ft. Kamehameha. The crew chief sat along side me in the NBS-1, a two-engined bomber, with the target operator in the rear. A few minutes after I had taken off that coal black night, I began a gentle left turn over the waters of Pearl Harbor and my left engine suddenly stopped. I cut the switch on that engine, opened up the other engine to full speed and leveled the plane. I wanted to stay over the water to avoid hitting an obstacle. My attention was completely taken up with maintaining flying speed although this meant losing altitude. I held my position until I caught a gleam of light on the water. I had only about ten feet altitude! As I pulled back on the throttle of the right engine to raise the nose of the plane, I hit the water in a perfect three-point landing. Immediately the nose started to sink and I checked with the other crew members to see if they were all right. The man in the rear cockpit shouted that he could not swim. I told him to climb out and get on the tail, which he did in nice shape. By this time our front cockpit was full of water, and we had to climb out to make our way toward the tail — still safely out of the water. We could hear a navy motor launch looking for us and kept shouting to it, but our voices seemed only to echo around the harbor. Soon our own Luke Field motor launch joined in the search with a searchlight, but it had no better luck until Lieutenant Alfred Hegenberger took off from the field in another bomber loaded with parachute flares. He dropped a series of them along our flight path, and with this help, the two boats readily located us and brought us to shore.

The Flight Surgeon Captain "Doc" Myers insisted on taking all three of us to the hospital for a checkup. After that Doc took me to his quarters, where a bridge game in progress apparently had not missed a beat during all the excitement. I phoned home to tell my wife I was okay and would spend the night with the Myers. Doc poured me a stiff drink of his medicinal whiskey and put me to bed. I slept like a baby.

The next morning I reported the details of the mishap to the Commanding Officer of Luke Field, Major Arnold Krogstad. A Navy derrick on a barge hauled the plane out of the water and left it at our shops for repair. I never did find out what caused the engine to quit.

THE MONTHS PASSED at Luke with routine missions in gunnery, bombing navigation, department maneuvers, and inter-island flights.

On one of these latter flights in one of our two-engine bombers to the Johnson Ranch on the island of Kauai, one engine threw a connecting rod, about ten miles off shore. We had sufficient altitude so I made an emergency landing northwest of the little town of Lihue. Lieutenant Jesse Madaraz was with me on this trip as a co-pilot and the crew chief rode in the rear cockpit.

About ten minutes after we landed, as Jesse and I were examining the damage, a young man came galloping up on horseback and asked if we were having trouble. I told him we would like to send a message back to Luke Field on Oahu, if he could do it. He agreed and also offered us a place to stay over.

About an hour later, as we were sitting under a wing of our plane, eating a box lunch which the mess had been good enough to put up for us, a two-horse wagon drove up. The driver asked if we were the "gemmen" he was supposed to carry up to the house.

We rode for about an hour along a dirt road and finally turned into the driveway of a beautiful big white frame house. The young man awaited us on the steps. We introduced ourselves. His name was Brodrero, and as he led us to our rooms, we passed a large case filled with battle flags of northern regiments from the Civil War. I asked our young host where the flags had come from and he said his grandfather had been a Brigadier General in the Confederate Army and his men had captured these flags.

After dinner we sat out on the front porch of the house and we learned the grandfather, an Italian count, had been a general in Garibaldi's Army. As the wars were coming to a close in Italy, he had emigrated to America with the idea of offering his services to the Union Army, but along the way someone had persuaded him to join the Confederate forces instead. After the war, the grandfather came to Honolulu and then to Kauai, where he bought from the King of Kauai much of the land comprising the Brodrero plantation. Our host's maternal grandfather, Colonel Z. N. Spaulding, had been a Civil War veteran on the Union side, commanding an Ohio regiment.

After an interesting and pleasurable week on the plantation, we received a message that the Navy tug with a new engine would soon arrive. During this week our crew chief had gone down to the plane and worked on disassembling the damaged engine to prepare for its removal.

With Brodrero's help we rented a truck to take the new engine from the port of Nawiliwili to the plane. Lieutenant Carl Cover, our Luke Field Engineering officer, and some mechanics came over on the tug to install the new engine. They finished the job quickly, and after thanking Mr. Brodrero we took off for Luke Field which we made before dark.

In December, 1970, I had occasion to return to Kauai. I wanted to visit the Valley House, Brodrero's home, applied to the Lihue Public Library for information as to its location. There I learned that the old House had been destroyed by fire on September 30, 1950.

XIX

1928-38: *Washington, Promotions, Command and General Staff School, Chennault and Spaatz*

⊛ AT THE END OF 1927 I returned to the states, under orders to report to the Chief of the Air Service's Office in Washington, D.C. Lt. Bob Worthington, a member of the 19th Squadron, had been killed in an airplane accident at Luke Field shortly before I left, so I served as escort officer for the body to San Francisco.

After leave with members of Eve's family in San Diego and a sea voyage on the Army transport San Mihiel through the Panama Canal to New York, we arrived in the Capitol in late February.

I spent two years with the Buildings and Grounds Division of the Chief's Office, working for Major Frank Kennedy, a pioneer flier and Air Service dirigible pilot; then I transferred to the Personnel Division of OCAS.

At this time there were 1,514 officers in the Air Service and yet there was no way of determining who had a specialty in engineering, communications, photography, supply and other important fields, nor was there a record of the service and specialty schools these officers had attended. I found that the Census Bureau had a key-punch card system in which such data could be filed and retrieved — similar to today's computer card system. I borrowed 2,000 cards and the Census Bureau's machine and punch, and processed all 1,514 officers so that when we had a call for an officer with a certain specialty, we could locate him quickly by running the cards through the machine.

Such a system sounds primitive today but it should be remembered that this all occurred in the early 1930's when the red tape and paperwork mills — the bureaucracy — still enjoyed its childhood. I remember a time when, searching for an important paper, I traced it down to the office of Capt. Frank "Monk" Hunter, serving on the staff of General William Gilmore, Chief of the Operations Divisions and Assistant Chief of the Air Service. Monk opened the bottom drawer of his desk and found my paper in a drawer full of correspondence. He explained that whenever he received a letter containing some inquiry he couldn't answer, he "filed" it in that drawer. Usually, he said, somebody solved the problem without his help anyway — or the problem solved itself.

Such a cavalier attitude would not be permitted today, I am sure.

In the period between 1931 until my first squadron command in 1938, I recall these special highlights:

WHILE AT MAXWELL FIELD, Alabama, in 1931, I participated in a three-ship formation, flying P-12's, with Capt. Claire Chennault, later of "Flying Tigers" fame, leading us. Before we left the ground, Chennault explained to us that in cross-over turns, which we were to practice, he as leader would dip his wing on the side to which we were to turn. Then the inside man would slide behind and below him, and the outside man would move above him. On one turn, Major Delos Emmons of San Francisco apparently did not see Chennault's dip-wing signal and as I slid over, I came within an eyelash of hitting him mid-air.

AT RANDOLPH FIELD, TEXAS, in 1932, in an effort to shed some bad flying habits, I joined a new flight class and went through the course with fresh young men. Lt. Homer Ferguson, a master pilot and a born instructor, guided me. I flew PT-1's and BT2's, primary and basic trainers, and this refresher course turned out to be among the real smart moves I made in my career.

AFTER A FLYING TRIP in 1933 with "Fergie" Ferguson to the Pacific Northwest, I returned and found myself promoted to Captain. In those days, we were all on a list and as vacancies occurred in a higher rank, we moved up the list and were promoted — the bad along with the good. The only qualification was being able to pass the physical.

IN 1936 I JOINED 159 other officers at Ft. Leavenworth, Kansas, for the Command and General Staff School — the teachings in which were, for the most part, a complete loss for me. The curriculum was designed for ground officers primarily and although our Air Corps instructor did a great job, an atmosphere of prejudice and ignorance of World War I vintage still existed toward military aviation. In the two years I spent at this school, only one instructor taught and examined us in what I considered a meaningful way about modern warfare. After completing this course and upon being ordered to Langley Field, Virginia, for my second tour there, I received notification of my promotion to temporary Major. At Langley, our Chief of Staff was Lt. Col. Carl Spaatz.

XX

1938-41: First Squadron Command, Submarine Patrol, Generals George Marshall, Henry "Hap" Arnold

IN SEPTEMBER, 1938, one year before the outbreak of war in Europe, Colonel Spaatz called me into his office at Langley and offered me the command of the 21st Reconnaissance Squadron. I accepted eagerly, although the unit had a poor reputation on the base and was pathetically equipped with a single B-18 in its single hangar at the south end of Langley Field.

After some preliminary weeding out of drunks, jailbirds, and chronic AWOL-ers, reducing the squadron strength by nearly half, I began working on both the manpower and materiel problems; stood up reasonably well under a thorough inspection by the Corps Area Inspector General, and received orders to ferry some new B-18's from the Douglas factory at Englewood, California, to the squadron.

For these flights, we were required to have logged 1,000 pilot-hours, so Captain James Fitzmaurice, my second-in-command of the 21st, joined me in ferrying the first plane back to Langley. On our arrival we found fifteen fresh second lieutenants had been assigned to our squadron, all newly graduated from flying school. We took one of these new officers as copilot on the remaining flights, checking them out on the B-18 en route. Soon we had our allotment of thirteen planes and were receiving good men from technical schools as mechanics and crew chiefs. After a course at the Air Corps Tactical School in Naval Operations at Maxwell Field, Montgomery, Alabama, early the next year I started transition training on the B-17. Captain Carl McDaniel of the 2nd Bomb Group was my instructor, and a fine one. Soon I received another experienced armament officer for the squadron in Lt. Jared V. Crabb, and with Fitzmaurice, Lt. Draper "Frew" Henry, and

Capt. Herbert Baisley, a photographic specialist, had a fine unit now, with full personnel and equipment, working hard on training schedules.

Around September 1, 1939, our squadron moved to the Miami Municipal Airport near Hialeah, to undertake submarine patrol of the Atlantic between Charleston, S.C., and Key West. To us, this sounded like the real thing, something for which we had been training. War had been declared in Europe between Germany and England that September 1, and we felt like we were getting prepared to take part.

Once settled in Miami — as settled as we could get in a half-completed camp, sleeping in the open and eating cold rations at the start — I laid out an operations schedule together with a training program for both flying and ground personnel, and we concentrated on night patrols since none of our young pilots had this experience.

General George C. Marshall paid us a visit during that winter of 1939 and gave us a very thorough inspection ,and later in the year, General Arnold also came down. After he inspected the squadron and our aircraft, we retired to the operations tent where I showed him the charts of our activities.

"How many AWOLs do you have, Craig?" he asked pointedly.

"None, sir," I answered.

He paused, surprised, then said, "What about your squadron's VD rate?"

"No VD, sir," I said, very coolly and truthfully.

Flabbergasted at this, he asked me how it could be true, what with Miami right next door to the camp. I explained that I lectured all recruites about venereal disease when they arrived and had my other officers repeat the lectures monthly to the whole squadron. I said I thought the men were too scared to expose themselves to the horrors of VD.

"You are doing a good job here," General Arnold said. "Keep up the good work."

Needless to say, we were all pleased at this parting shot.

One Sunday morning one of our planes on patrol spotted a German freighter offshore at Ft. Lauderdale, north of Miami, and radioed the news to the field. Two British warships were giving the German vessel chase. I ordered the plane to keep the German under surveillance, then took off to see what was happening. When I arrived off Ft. Lauderdale, the British were firing on the German ship which, in turn, was steaming fast for the shore. Just before it went aground, it made a hard port turn and entered Port Everglades. The British remained offshore for several days to keep the freighter bottled up.

I returned to the field and called the officer in charge of the Naval Air Base and asked him to meet me at the Port Everglades dock to go aboard the German ship. After sending a wire to the Naval District at Charleston, we went aboard and met the German captain and his officers (plus one civilian who appeared to be in charge). I notified them they were now interned and that no one could leave the ship. On my orders, a sentry stood guard at the bottom of the gangplank. When I returned to camp a message from the Charleston Naval District ordered me to turn the whole affair over to the Port Collector at Tampa. The ship remained in port for the duration of the war.

Late in the summer of 1941, orders arrived relieving me of command of the 21st squadron and assigning me, once again, to the Chief's Office in Washington. I was very much touched at the farewell tribute the squadron gave me.

When I reported for duty in Washington, I found my assignment was with the Air War Plans Division. Among my first duties, I aided Colonel Joseph McNarney of the Army General Staff, in helping lay out air routes across the Pacific — urgent work since B-17s would soon be sent out to reinforce the Philippines.

The work lasted several weeks and finally I drafted a directive to the Commanding General, Hawaii, of the Army, instructing him to proceed with developing air bases and alloting him $10 million for that purpose. The Navy seemed very reluctant to cooperate in this undertaking. They did not believe land planes should be flying over great water expanses such as the Pacific. Secretly, I thought they opposed our entering what they believed to be their private ocean.

By the time this work was completed, some changes had taken place in the command of the Air War Plans Division: in a nutshell, I found myself in charge of the division at a time when finishing touches were being placed on a plan known as "AWPD-1" — a plan to fight the air war against Germany.

XXI

1942: Air Routes and Island-Hopping

WHEN PEARL HARBOR EXPLODED under Japanese attack, we plunged directly into the War. General Arnold, anxious to develop air routes to England, Russia and the British forces in Egypt, assigned me to this job. With England having first priority and its air route starting at the aircraft factories in California and thence in a great circle course over some subarctic areas, I had to find some arctic advisors, men who had lived in such areas and who knew the conditions from personal experience. I got in touch with Viljhalmur Stefansson, the renowned Arctic explorer, in New York, and he gave me the names and addresses of a group he thought would be suitable. Among them were William Carlson, who became my assistant in Arctic matters in the office, and Bernt Balchen. Balchen was engaged at the time in the delivery of flying boats from the factory in San Diego to Australia. When he reported in, I explained the project to him, told him we would commission him a captain, and said his first job would be to supervise the building of an air base in Greenland. He said, "Fine," and went down to the dispensary in the Pentagon to take his physical examination. He was found to have double hernia which the doctors told him would have to be repaired before he could receive his commission. He asked what they were waiting for and they sent him up to Walter Reed Hospital for the operation. Three days later he was back in my office, ready to go to work. He received his captaincy and departed for New York, where a ship was being loaded with materials for building an air base in Greenland. Balchen, who went with the ship, contractors, materials and engineers, soon had the base functioning at Bluie West Eight on the west side of Greenland.

Carlson proved to be a real find and a strong right arm to me. A college teacher when I called him in and commissioned him, he sorted out the people who wanted in on the Arctic project, and he personally determined the suitability and usefulness for air bases of locations we picked from our maps. We established bases at Great Falls, Montana (also used to supply Alaska and the Russians); Churchill, Canada; Fort Chimo, on Ungava Bay; Baffin Island; Bluie West Eight, at Sandrestorm Fjord on the west coast of Greenland; Angmagssalik, on the east coast of Greenland; Reykjavik in Iceland, and then in England.

I cannot express enough praise for the people we selected to man these out-of-the-way places. They did a magnificent job, and too little credit has been given to them. Bernt Balchen, for example, led rescue parties for planes which had gone down on the Greenland ice cap. When our field at Fort Chimo burned to the ground, no one was hurt. These men solved tremendous supply problems. The only ship we could lay our hands on for the job on the east coast of Greenland was a refrigerated fruit ship, painted white. It first went to Iceland and then, with the help of our Coast Guard vessels, managed to reach Angmagssalik on the east coast of Greenland and unload. Later we found this station superfluous and closed it, except for weather observations.

Another air route we established began at Palm Beach, Florida, and proceeded down through the West Indies and British Guiana to Natal, Brazil, thence across the South Atlantic to Ascension Island and Accra, Africa. Across Africa the planes flew to Khartoum on the Nile River, and up the Nile to Cairo. From here the route extended across Jordan and Iraq to Teheran in Iran, where the planes were turned over to the Russians.

Yet another route was mapped from Great Falls, Montana, up through western Canada to Fairbanks, Alaska, where the Russians took delivery of most of the planes and flew them on to Nome and thence across Siberia. General Arnold tried his very best to persuade the Russians to permit us to deliver the aircraft directly to Russia, but he never succeeded. He also tried to get their permission to deliver directly the planes sent to Teheran, but had no luck with this proposal either.

One Sunday morning in March, 1942, while I was working in my office, General Arnold sent for me. Colonel David Grant, our chief medical officer, was with General Arnold when I got there, so I sat down on a bench in the outside waiting room, soon joined by Colonel Steve Ferson of Operations. A heavyset man, much overweight, Ferson's trip to Arnold's office had him sweating profusely and out of breath. Grant soon came out through the swinging halfdoors leading to Arnold's office, and the secretary went in. In a few minutes she emerged to say General Arnold wanted to see Colonel Ferson now. Ferson went into the office. I heard a thump, followed by a yell from General Arnold. When I ran in, General Arnold was pointing to Steve Ferson, lying stretched out on the floor. I dashed to the hall door and whistled for the Dave Grant to come back in on the double. When he had examined Ferson, he straightened up and faced General Arnold. "He is dead, and if you don't start taking things easier, you will be right behind him. Now, how about closing this office for the day and going home?" General Arnold did exactly that. All of us were shaken.

Soon after this incident, I served on a board of officers, with General Harry J. Maloney as chairman, to select the sites and lay out runway directions for airfields in Bermuda, and other islands in the West Indies and British Guiana. President Roosevelt had arranged with Prime Minister Churchill to exchange a number of our overage destroyers for these fields.

While we were in Puerto Rico, General Maloney arranged with our Navy to furnish me a destroyer which would take me down through the string of islands. I left the next day and we stopped first at Antigua where I checked in with the Administrator of the island. We soon had a site selected and the runway directions proposed for a field which still is being used today.

At the next port, St. Lucia, the Administrator met me and cooperated beautifully with the problems on my hands. He asked me to have dinner with him and some of his officials that night. I accepted and found myself the only white person at the table, all the others being local blacks. At St. Vincent I checked in with the Governor of the Windward Islands, and from there, we proceeded to Trinidad. This island had an airfield already, but General Andrews had sent a team from Panama to select another site, and work was already underway on new Waller Field. I met the other members of the Board at Trinidad and told General Maloney of my visits to Antigua, St. Lucia and St. Vincent.

Georgetown, the capital of British Guiana, my last stop, up the Demerara River a little bit, and the destroyer skipper was afraid to chance it so he put me ashore in a small boat. At the dock to meet me was an American, an Air Corps Reserve Officer pilot who ran a charter air service out of Georgetown. When I explained what I needed, he said he knew just the place. We got aboard another launch and went up the river about ten miles. The soil on the proposed site had a sandy texture, unusual for a jungle region. My American friend assured me that the area would be large enough for two runways and the necessary buildings. When we returned to Georgetown, he fetched a map and marked out the location of the airfield and plotted the runways. I later turned this map over to the Engineer on the Board, Colonel Dogan Arthur, with a recommendation that the site be developed. It became one of the most successful locations of them all — Atkinson Field Hydroponic Station, so named for the water-grown vegetables there.

Back in Washington, I wrote up the entire proceedings and sent them to General Maloney.

XXII

1942: Bolero, Roundup; Mission to England

☆ SHORTLY AFTER THIS island-hopping expedition, in April, 1942, while having a meeting with my section chiefs to find out what was going on in the Division, my "squawk-box" buzzed. General Arnold, on the other end, asked how long it would take me to get down to his office. I said, "Two minutes," and he said, "Make it one!"

When I arrived, he asked me if I had ever heard of *Bolero* or *Roundup*. When I answered negatively, he responded: "You'd better find out all you can about them — and quickly. Talk to Ed Hull." Major General Hull, a classmate of mine for two years while we were at Ft. Leavenworth, at this time was Chief of the Operations Division of the War Department General Staff. General George C. Marshall, the Chief of Staff of the Army, used this division as his Command Post, and the War Plans Section was one of its big divisions. Hull told me I would soon depart on a very secret mission with General Marshall — not to mention this to anyone, not even my wife, and that I would be gone about two weeks. (My dear wife, being an "army brat," took it in stride.)

Hull instructed me to come back at two o'clock, and he would have a team from the WPD brief me on *Bolero* and *Roundup*. Present at the briefing were Hull, Al Wedemeyer, another Leavenworth classmate, two briefers and I, and the session lasted three hours. I learned that *Bolero* was the code word for the build up of American Forces — Air, Land and Sea — in the British Isles of more than a million men, to be completed by mid-summer of 1943, when the plan to invade the continent of Europe, known then as *Roundup*, would be put into operation. Both plans had been approved by the Joint Chiefs of Staff and the President. During the buildup period of *Bolero*, air and naval operations against the Germans were to be intensified in order to destroy or neutralize their defense forces and installations and to give some relief to the Russians.

I asked how many air groups and what kind of fighters, heavy bombers, medium and light bombers, reconnaissance aircraft and others we expected to place in Great Britain before *Roundup* began, and Wedemeyer said that as General Muir Fairchild, our airman on the Joint Planning Staff, was handling all Army Air matters, I would have to see him. Admiral Forrest Sherman had charge of all Navy Air Matters.

I returned to General Arnold's office with a fair idea of the nature of the two plans, and suggested to him that there appeared to be a complete absence of anything resembling an air program. Arnold put me in touch with General Fairchild who could not have been more cooperative, turning everything he had relating to *Bolero* and *Roundup* over to me, together with his own notebooks with details on the military buildup in Britain. I asked Fairchild why the Old Man didn't send him on this mission, inasmuch as he had been living with the two plans for months while I had entered the picture cold. He shrugged his shoulders and said nothing. Later, I learned that Fairchild was in the doghouse with Arnold at that particular time. I never did find out why.

We were to leave the United States for England on April 4, 1942. All references to the mission — telephone, radio, cable, correspondence and documents — would be identified by the word MODICUM, which means "a little." Fictitious names were assigned to each of us for the purpose of secrecy. They were as follows:

Mr. Harry Hopkins to be known as Mr. A. A. Hones.

General Marshall to be known as Mr. C. G. Mell.

Commander James R. Fulton to be known as Mr. A. L. Foss.

Colonel H. A. Craig to be known as Mr. J. H. Case.

Lt. Colonel A. C. Wedemeyer to be known as Mr. J. E. White.

THE RESPONSIBILITY for all flight arrangements to and from England fell on my shoulders. We were told to wear civilian clothes and to carry no uniforms.

The Adjutant General delivered the orders personally to each of us and gave us additional instructions as follows: Al Wedemeyer and I were told to go to Baltimore by car on the evening of April 3 to a certain hotel and to take a seat in the lobby. We were not to check in but wait until we were paged. About five minutes after our arrival, I heard a "Mr. J. H. Case" being paged but it made no impression on me. After a little while a "Mr. J. E. White" was paged, and after a few calls it suddenly occurred to Al that *he* was "J. E. White." He answered the call and met near the door a Pan-American Airways representative, who told us to check into the hotel. After depositing our luggage in our rooms, the PAA representative asked us to meet him in the lobby, where he informed us of the arrangements for the trip and the location of the Boeing Clipper-type flying boat in which we would cross the Atlantic. After a few hours sleep in the hotel, we hurried downstairs to a PAA car, waiting to take us to the pier where the Clipper had moored. There we met Captain Harold Gray, the pilot (now a senior vice president of PAA in charge of all operations), Captain Arthur L. McCullough (who later came into the Air Transport Command of the Air Forces and remained in the service until he retired as a Brigadier General in 1955), and eleven crew members. We had a good breakfast and at 6:30 A.M. a White House car drove up with General Marshall, Harry Hopkins and a Commander Fulton.

Our luggage aboard, we were ready to taxi to the middle of the Chesapeake Bay for take-off. It surprised me to see General Marshall in uniform when we had been told so explicitly to wear civilian clothes. Harry Hopkins headed for one of the lower berths and turned in. General Marshall then told Al and me that Hopkins had been in poor health and that President Roosevelt hoped all of us would protect him as much as possible, not only against the arduous trip but also against himself, for he had a penchant for driving himself too hard. Commander Fulton, an outstanding doctor and Hopkins' personal physician, turned out to be a delightful traveling companion.

Soon we were in the air, on our way to Bermuda, 750 miles distant.

About halfway there, while General Marshall, Wedemeyer, Fulton and I were having a snack lunch, a terrific vibration went through the plane which lasted only a few seconds. General Marshall asked me what caused the noise, and I suggested that one of the pilots had opened his cockpit window. I had such an experience before. As soon as we finished our lunch, Captain McCullough appeared at the door of the flight deck and indicated he wanted to see me. I joined him on the flight deck and Captain Gray asked me if I had seen what happened. I stared at him, questioning, and he pointed to number 2 engine, which had its propeller feathered and a big hole in the side of the crankcase where the piston and connecting rod had gone through.

He asked whether we ought to continue to Bermuda or turn back to New York. I asked him if they had a spare engine in Bermuda and upon contacting the island we learned they did have a *stripped* spare engine which meant that the accessories would have to be removed from the damaged engine and installed on the spare. I told Gray to be sure to use the word MODICUM in all his radio messages, and asked him to send a message to the "Senior Naval Officer Present" (SNOP) at Bermuda, requesting assistance in the form of labor and material to expedite the changing of engines and sign it MODICUM. He suggested that he send another message to PAA NEW YORK to alert them in the event we ran into some unforseeable trouble.

Returning to the cabin, I explained to General Marshall and Hopkins what had happened, the messages we had sent to Bermuda, the replies, and my decision to proceed to Bermuda, rather than turn back to New York. This startled General Marshall and he asked *"You decided?"* I outlined my reasoning: the secrecy of the mission, the fact that we would have plenty of help from the Navy, weather conditions would probably be better leaving from Bermuda, and the fact that the next day was Easter Sunday when other arrangements would be difficult to make. He asked when I thought we would be able to leave and I said Monday evening at the latest. He finally gave his blessings, and Harry Hopkins said "Good boy."

We arrived over Bermuda about noon. I had been there before of course, as the junior member of the Board implementing the Destroyer-Air Base deal which FDR had arranged with Churchill. At that time, our Board had experienced considerable difficulty with the island's Governor-General, an old fellow who would have no part permitting motor vehicles on the island, let alone the building of air base there. We got nowhere with him and when we returned to Washington, we had to report his recalcitrant attitude. He was promptly relieved of his job, and a new Governor-General assigned, so we did not anticipate having our former problems repeated.

We were met at the pier on Darrell Island by Admiral James (SNOP) of the U.S. Navy, who had a detail of men and several machine shop trucks ready to start work. An aide to the Governor-General also met us and we were put up at the Belmont Manor Hotel where the accommodations were excellent. At the hotel we found invitations for dinner with the Governor-General, Lord and Lady Knoles, at the palace. During dinner, among other things ,many jokes were made of the secrecy of our mission. Apparently everyone on the island knew who we were and precisely why we were going to England.

Our original flight plan had called for an early departure on Easter Sunday; however, departure time had to be set back to Monday to permit the installation of the new engine. When the Governor-General discovered that the MODICUM party would be in Bermuda for another twenty-four hours at least, he invited General Marshall to read the second lesson at the Easter services in the local English church. It is a tradition in the territories of the British Empire and the Commonwealth to ask the senior civil official to read the First Lesson and the senior military personage present to read the Second Lesson.

On our way back to the hotel from the Governor-General's palace that evening, General Marshall instructed Al Wedemeyer to get in touch with the aide and find out what passage he would be expected to read. He said he had been caught in situations like this before, faced with reading a lot of unpronounceable names. At the hotel, Al called the aide (probably a Yorkshireman) who had a severe accent. Al learned that General Marshall would be expected to read Chapter 1, Verses 1-8 of the Book of Revelation. Then, with the assistance of the hotel staff we began hunting for a Bible. Finally someone remembered an old lady housekeeper who lived in one of the attic rooms of the hotel. We all charged up the stairs, probably scaring the poor soul half to death, but she had a Bible, well worn with use, which Al persuaded her to lend to us.

We went up to General Marshall's sitting room and found him talking to Harry Hopkins. Al read from his note the lesson which the Governor's aide had said would be the General's lesson and Marshall said he would read it aloud and we were to criticize. After hearing him read the Scripture, we were all satisfied that he would do fine. After breakfast the next morning, I told General Marshall I would like to go to the services at the Catholic Church, and did not know if I would get out in time to join him for the English Church services. He said that would be perfectly all right. I learned later from Al that, unfortunately, he had misunderstood the information given to him by Lord Knole's aide. Instead of Verses 1-8, General Marshall was expected to read Verses 1-18. Al did not discover the error until he read it on the announcement board in the church, and was too far away to warn General Marshall that there were some real tongue-twisters in those additional ten verses. However, the general managed to get through all eighteen verses by dropping his voice to a whisper when the tongue-twisters (Ephesus, Pergamos, Thyatira, Laodicea) came along. One word struck a responsive chord, and he almost shouted "Philadelphia" when it appeared.

XXIII

1942: Bermuda to Ireland

AFTER LUNCH that Easter Sunday, Harry Hopkins asked me if I could show him a projection of our aircraft production and allotments to our Allies for the next year. The charts on these subjects I had received from General Arnold, who impressed on me that I would not show them to the British or make any copies of them, but memorize the information they contained. Anyway, I retrieved the charts from the hotel safe and spread them out on the floor of Hopkins' sitting room. Then we got down on our knees and went over them, item by item, talking about units, how many groups would be allotted to Europe or the Pacific, how many squadrons in the various groups, how many airplanes in each squadron and their characteristics — speed, radius of action, altitude. General Marshall came in the room when we were discussing the number of squadrons in a group, whereupon he suddenly left and returned in a few minutes with a black book which he said General Arnold had given him. He asked me, "How many squadrons are in a group of, say, bombers?" I told him three. He said Arnold's book indicated four. I told him it *had* been four until about a month ago, and probably General Arnold had not had time to change it, explaining my information came from Fairchild's black book. General Marshall said this was too important a matter to be left to debate, and that he was not at all sure. He wanted me to send the following message to General Arnold, priority, "Craig says there are three squadrons in a group. Your book says four. Who is right?" I did not have the slightest idea of how to send a classified message from Bermuda.

Our session on the floor of Hopkins' room proved to be a good dry run for me, and as I placed the charts again in the hotel safe, Al Wedemeyer came in the lobby and said he had been out to our plane, readied for takeoff the next day. When I told him about my problem of sending the message, he suggested we call up General George Strong, the American Commanding General, who would be charged with the defense of the island air base upon its completion. General Strong had a message for me, when we arrived is his office, a message from the British Air Ministry, directing us to delay our departure for twenty-four hours with no reason given. I suggested to Marshall and Hopkins the reason might be bad weather in the British Isles; Hopkins thought it might be for security reasons. I informed Captain Gray of the directed delay, and on my way back to the hotel stopped at the home of the American Consul General who was giving a cocktail party for MODICUM. Our mission had been rightly named because practically all of the island officialdom and socialdom were on hand — and the secrecy of our mission was minimal.

That night before we retired, Harry Hopkins asked us to meet him in his sitting room. When we were all present, he said that on his previous trips to London, he was shocked at lack of fresh fruits and vegetables available to the British people. He suggested that we all donate $5.00 or so, and one of us could go down to the market and buy a couple of crates of these commodities to give to the Prime Minister. He said he knew that Mary Churchill, the PM's daughter, would immediately take over and distribute it to hospitals or orphan homes, and he knew that the Prime Minister would appreciate the gesture. General Marshall approved the project and designated Wedemeyer to take care of it. I might say here that General Marshall had not been in England since World War I; Al Wedemeyer was there for a short visit when he graduated from the German War College early in 1939; neither Commander Fulton or I had ever been there; Harry Hopkins had made several trips to London from the time Lend Lease started in 1940.

The next day, Monday, General Marshall and Harry Hopkins went fishing. Al, Dr. Fulton and I went on a shopping expedition and tour of Hamilton, Bermuda. We left Al at the market to buy the fruit and vegetables and to arrange for the delivery of the crates to the Clipper.

That evening we all had a quiet dinner together at the hotel, and talked until nearly midnight. Earlier in the evening, we received a message from General Arnold, and may God bless his soul, he said that Craig was right, there were *three* squadrons to a group, and apologized for not bringing his book up-to-date. General Marshall never used Arnold's black book after that, as far as I know.

A phone call shortly after midnight explained that all arrangements were firm for our scheduled departure. (Later in the war, we would have considered this to be a very serious violation of security.) We were up at 4 A.M., ate breakfast, packed our belongings and took the transportation provided for us to the pier on Darrell Island. At the pier there stood a large contingent of both Amercian and British officials to see us off — another indication of the lack of security.

Our pilot briefed us to the effect that we had a straight over water flight of 3,000 miles or about 20 hours flying time. Our ship grossed at 88,000 pounds, carrying 5,300 gallons of fuel. In flight the plane consumed about 50 gallons per engine or 200 gallons an hour. We would land in Lock Erne in North Ireland.

Our takeoff was uneventful and a short time after gaining altitude, we struck a front which had considerable turbulence. After about three hours of lurching, creaking and generally rough going, the air suddenly smoothed out. That evening we went to bed in comfortable berths, equal to those found in the most luxurious Pullmans on the American railroads.

I awakened about 4 A.M., dressed and shaved and had a cup of coffee from one of the stewards — the last good cup I would receive for some time — and went up to the flight deck and asked Captain Gray for permission to come aboard, which he smilingly granted. It was just breaking daylight and we were off Ireland, under British radar surveillance. We made it direct to Loch Erne, landing straight ahead, and taxied up to the pier. This was a Coastal Command Station of the R.A.F. engaged in antisubmarine patrol. We had breakfast with some of the officers at the station, while our baggage was transferred to a land plane at a nearby base.

We were carried over to the adjoining airfield in Irish jaunting carts. Soon we were aloft again in an eight-seater transport, ample for the five of us and two Royal Air Force officers who accompanied our group.

Just before we left the seaplane station, I had a few minutes with Captain Gray to ask him about his plans. As soon as he had refueled, he planned to leave for Preswick, Scotland, where I could get in touch with him through Air Force operations. He asked that I keep him advised of our approximate departure time.

On our way to London, we were escorted by fighters off each wing, to the rear and overhead. As we crossed the Irish Sea, we saw a convoy moving northward, well protected by destroyers and air cover. Gradually, we were being exposed to the grim realities of war.

To Maj. Gen. "Punky" Craig,
One of the group upon whom I relied
so much to carry the load while building
up our Air Force. Best regards

XXIV

1942: Sir Alan Brook and the British Imperial Staff

WE ARRIVED at the Croydon Airport outside London about
1 P.M., April 8, to be met by Prime Minister Churchill and
the British Chiefs of Staff. After a brief but warm welcome,
we were whisked off to Claridge's Hotel in the Heart of London.

I will always believe that every one of our rooms in the Claridge
had been thoroughly "bugged," although the thought did not occur
to me until many months later. I shared these same rooms with Generals Eisenhower and Mark Clark in June, 1942, and later when General Carl Spaatz arrived with his staff, they were installed in exactly
the same suite. All of us were truly "innocents abroad."

General Marshall gave us the afternoon off to see some of our
friends, but that evening we had a dry run on what he would say to
the British Chiefs the next day.

General Marshall, Al Wedemeyer and I were awaked early by a
valet who, I am sure, was member of British Intelligence. He helped
to arrange my clothes and also ordered breakfast, which consisted of
two pieces of stringy, tough bacon, rubbery mushrooms, toast and the
most awful coffee I have ever tasted.

A little before ten o'clock the three of us left for the British War
Cabinet offices for our initial conference. We were met there by General James Chaney, Air Corps, who headed the U.S. Mission to Great
Britain, Admiral Ghormeley, the senior U.S. Naval officer in London,
and Brigadier General Robert A. McClure, an attaché of the Army and
another Leavenworth classmate. I did not realize then how important
this meeting was to be to me later — when General Eisenhower asked
me to accompany him to his initial encounter with the British Chiefs

of Staff and to brief him on the drill and the personalities of each of them.

After an exchange of pleasantries and a warm expression of welcome by Sir Alan Brooke, the Chief of the Imperial General Staff who acted as Chairman, General Marshall made a few introductory remarks concerning the strategic situation as we Americans saw it. He outlined in a broad, general way our proposals for allied operations in the European area during the remainder of 1942 and on through 1943. General Brooke, after making a few comments in reply, was followed by Admiral Louis Mountbatten, Sir Charles Portal, the Air Chief, and Sir Dudley Pound of the British Navy.

The meeting broke up about noon, and we were invited to have luncheon with the British as guests of Sir Alan Brooke. When we assembled at the Savoy Hotel, General Marshall asked Al and me to visit the Combined Operations Headquarters which had recently been organized under Admiral Mountbatten. He cautioned us not to commit ourselves on anything but for Al to be prepared to give him a complete resume later.

At the combined operations headquarters that afternoon, Admiral Mountbatten introduced us to his key men: young admirals, generals and air marshals, all of whom impressed me very favorably. The Admiral then explained his organization, coordination and planning and the objects he had under investigation.

There is no doubt that combined operations performed a great service during the war. The organization was responsible for the development of many valuable but sometimes weird contraptions, and many important innovations in modern warfare were developed and introduced by this organization.

That evening Al reported to General Marshall our experience with the Combined Operations Headquarters, and Marshall asked Wedemeyer for his opinion and estimate of the British JCS. This was right down Al's alley; he had probably been thinking about it all day. He started off by describing Sir Alan Brooke as "very cautious" as he commented on the American concept. But, Al pointed out, this was natural in view of the British technique of negotiating, masters in the use of words and phrases which carried more than one meaning or interpretation. He said he did not suggest that the will to deceive was a personal characteristic of any of the participants, but that when matters of State were involved, our British opposite numbers had elastic scruples: to skim over or skip the facts for King and Country was justified in the consciences of these British gentlemen.

Al was quick to point out to General Marshall that there had been no expressed opposition to the American position at this first meeting, just polite suggestions that there might be difficulties in the undertaking of this task and that. What Wedemeyer suggested involved the British power of diplomatic finesse in its finest form, a power that had been developed over centuries of successful international intrigue, cajolery and tacit compulsions. He said at the morning meeting he sat reflecting upon the history of the British as he watched their senior military leaders carefully parrying, sidestepping and avoiding a head-on collision at this stage of the conference. Certainly, he thought, the British were in a desperate situation; however, nothing in their demeanor appeared to reveal concern or doubt about the final victory.

He described the session as his first experience with trained negotiators, negotiators who had a great tradition and were familiar hands at using intimidation of latent force or resorting to subtle deals — doing anything and everything to protect and extend British interests. Throughout British history those interests had generally been linked to the fostering of trade. Although we had become partners for an identical purpose — to defeat the Germans, Italians and Japanese — Al felt that we must realize that the British had certain ulterior motives or national aims to satisfy. We Americans, adolescents in the international field, had no clear-cut conception of our own national interest. Wedemeyer proceeded in this manner: "We wanted to crush our enemies militarily, making the world safe for Democracy, and protect the Four Freedoms, but as I watched the British Chiefs of Staff in action this morning, I was impressed once again that we had no definite National Aims.

"With regard to the British Chiefs as individuals, I sensed in Sir Alan Brooke a quick, incisive mind. He was articulate, sensitive, one who would not quibble at the necessity of coming to grips frontally with a basic issue.

"Sir Dudley Pound was a typical British Navy officer — a gentleman, courteous, a twinkle in his clear blue eyes, a florid complexion, small in stature, large in his grasp of humanity and at times rather taciturn. I liked particularly his statement this morning, when he was asked if he had any comment to make on the proposals. He replied, 'Thank God, someone wants to fight!' Although he might give the impression of not following closely the subject matter when asked to comment, he proved to be mentally alert and completely in the picture.

"Sir Charles Portal, the Air Chief, with his large nose and high forehead, presented an unusual picture. If you noticed, he seldom raised his eyes, and when he spoke, it was evident that he used considerable care in choosing his words. Evidently he has a great capacity for the formulation and expression of ideas. There was never a tinge of resentment or smugness about him, and he seemed to weigh the other person's viewpoint in an intelligent and sympathetic manner without weakening his own position. I thought that Sir Charles was a notch or two above the other members of the British Chiefs of Staff, as far as character and all-around intellectual capacity were concerned.

"Admiral Mountbatten is by all odds the most colorful of the British Chiefs. He is charming, tactful, a gallant knight in shining armor, handsome, bemedaled, with a tremendous amount of self-assurance. Because of his youthfulness, which was emphasized by his appearance, it was obvious that the older officers did not defer readily to his views. They seemed to be careful, however, to give him a semblance of courteous attention, because after all, he was a cousin of the King and, no doubt about it, a favorite of the Prime Minister.

"Although not a member of the British Chiefs of Staff Organization, Sir Hastings Ismay, as the Prime Minister's military secretary, attended all of their meetings. He appeared to me to be a 'smoothie.' He has a talent for ingratiating himself and obviously enjoyed the aura which surrounded his position of proximity to the Prime Minister. I judged him to be insincere, a man without real convictions and incapable of reaching sound conclusions. He seemed to be cast in the role of 'Mr.

Fix-it,' of spreading oil on troubled waters and alleviating difficult situations for the PM."

I sat spellbound listening to Al, admiring the manner in which he expressed himself. General Marshall then asked me if I had anything to add to Al's presentation to which I had to say, "No, sir. I think that it was complete and a fair estimate for a first meeting and I agree with it." General Marshall then thanked us and told us we could go.

Afterwards, I only hoped that the British had the records on their "bugs" for this dissertation. I am sure there would have been many red ears around Whitewall if this were the case.

After a hearty breakfast the next morning at the American mess, we returned to Claridge's to pick up some papers that were waiting for us from General Chaney's Headquarters. While there, I received a telephone call from the Secretary of State for Air, Sir Archibald Sinclair. He asked me to come down to the Air Ministry for a conference with the R.A.F. senior planners; he would send a car for me right away. I told him of my scheduled meeting that morning with the Joint Staff Planners. Sir Archibald said he knew that the Joint Staff Planners would be discussing ground and naval forces this morning, and that Air Commodore Elliot of the R.A.F., of the Joint Staff Planners would be attending *his* meeting. I went up to General Marshall's room, where he was talking to Harry Hopkins, and explained the situation to him. Marshall asked Hopkins how Sinclair fitted into the picture. When Hopkins explained Sinclair's position in the Government, General Marshall told me to go ahead with him. I relayed his approval to the Secretary, who said a car would be right down to pick me up. I felt very apprehensive about this meeting, because I knew I would be up against some real air experts and professional planners.

XXV

1942: A No. 10 Downing Street Meeting

✦ AFTER THE INTRODUCTIONS, Secretary Sinclair asked me to give in broad terms the outline plans for *Bolero* and *Roundup*. But before I could begin, an orderly arrived in the room to notify Sir Archibald of a phone call. He never returned to the meeting. Much later, I realized that the Air Ministry was using his title as a front for them.

I gave the planners a general outline of the way we were thinking for *Bolero* and *Roundup*. The discussion started off with the premise that something should be done and this was the first tangible idea yet presented. Then the planners began asking what air power we could contribute to the operation, and I had to be very cagey. They asked for the radius of action of our new P-47 fighter, its ceiling and bomb load. I had to tell them that we had been having a little trouble with the P-47 — its ailerons had a habit of blowing off — but we thought that we should soon have it fixed.

Innumerable questions followed, the main issue being on the number of squadrons we would have for *Bolero* and *Roundup*. Finally we adjourned for lunch, and Air Marshall John Slessor, who after the War became Chief of the Royal Air Force, took me to the R.A.F. Club, where we had a fairly decent meal. After lunch we resumed the talks — a tough session for me — but finally I think the planners got the idea that I was not putting out any definite figures.

General Marshall, Harry Hopkins and Al had been invited to Checkers, Churchill's country home, for the weekend. I was left out for some unknown reason, but it proved very fortunate for me. On Friday night an old friend of mine, Colonel Eddie Aldrin (the father of our present-day astronaut) an engineer with Shell Oil and then on active duty as a reserve officer, came around to the hotel to see me. He said if we were going to have all the air forces we were talking about operating out of England, we surely would need a Depot Organization of some kind for maintenance, supply and repair. He said that the R.A.F. had a fine new layout, unoccupied, at Burtonwood, near Liverpool. He thought that if I had nothing else to do, we ought to go up and look it over. The next day, Saturday, we got an airplane and flew up to Burtonwood.

A Royal Air Force Wing Commander met us and drove us all around. It was an ideal place to start a Service Command for the maintenance, repair, and supply of our Air Force. I asked him what plans the R.A.F. had for the place, and he said, as far as he knew, none. When I asked him if he thought the R.A.F. would consider turning the place over to the American Air Force, he said he knew of no reason why they should not.

The next day, Eddie Aldrin and I went down to the Air Ministry in Whitehall and started out with the party the Wing Commander at Burtonwood had named as the man to see. From this person, we went up the scale, until about four o'clock in the afternoon, we had Burtonwood signed, sealed and delivered.

Afterward, I learned from Al Wedemeyer that the crates of fruits and vegetables that he had bought in Bermuda had been delivered to the Prime Minister's home at Checkers. On Sunday morning, the PM called the MODICUM party together and had the gardener open the crates. To Al's dismay and embarrassment, the crates contained only brussel sprouts, the one vegetable in abundant supply in Britain. Churchill laughed and soon everyone joined in.

Monday was another all day session with the Planners, without any lunch, and I had the impression they were running shifts on us. The next day we attended a briefing by the British Intelligence Agencies at the War Office in the morning and another session with the Joint Staff Planners in the afternoon. This turned out to be our last session with the British Planners.

That evening of the 14th, General Marshall met with the Defense Cabinet to decide on final action, and the next evening we left London by train to witness some field exercises. The comfortable compartments gave each of a chance to get some much needed rest. On our return to London on the 17th, Marshall and Hopkins had a last-minute conference with the Prime Minister.

EARLY ON SATURDAY, the 18th, while I packed my bags, General Marshall came into my room, to say the Prime Minister wanted to see me right away and that a car awaited me in the front of the hotel. Flabbergasted, I wondered aloud why the Prime Minister would want to see *me*. Marshall said he did not know but that I had better get started and Wedemeyer would finish my packing. They would hold the plane until I returned.

I took off, and sure enough a big black limousine had parked at the door of the hotel. I got into it, did not say a word to the chauffeur and finally wound up at the door of No. 10 Downing Street. I identified myself to the policeman at the door who picked up a phone and said, "Colonel Craig is here." The door opened in a few moments and I followed another police officer down — and I mean *down* — a long narrow corridor, finally stopping at a door upon which the policeman knocked. It was opened by a very plain looking woman — in her fifties, I judged — who, I learned later, served as one of the PM's secretaries. Before I knew it, I stood in the bedroom of Prime Minister Winston Spencer Churchill.

He lay in bed and had on his head an old-fashioned nightcap with a tassel on the end. On his stomach, outside of the covers, lounged a huge Siamese cat. At the head of the bed stood a cooler containing a magnum of champagne. I introduced myself, saying I was with General Marshall's party and understood the Prime Minister wanted to see me. He said, "Yes, sit down." As I sat, the cat jumped on my lap. I took him by the scruff of the neck and put him on the floor. Churchill asked, "You don't like cats?" I said no and he responded, "Well, you are going to like that cat while you are here." Fortunately, the cat made no further advances towards me.

The Prime Minister then said, "General Marshall tells me you are in charge of the return flight to America. Tell me your itinerary."

I said, "Mr. Prime Minister, I am afraid I can't. I haven't seen or contacted the captain of the plane since we landed in Northern Ireland. Principally for security reasons."

Churchill looked at me and said calmly, "I can understand that. But once you get in touch with the plane, what do you suppose the course will be?"

At this point all I could venture was an educated guess, as I did not have the latest information on flying conditions. I thought that we would leave Preswick, in Scotland, and land at Gander Lake in Newfoundland. He said that from all the information he had, Gander would be frozen solid at this time of the year. (He tricked me on this one because I have since learned that Gander never freezes.) I went on to say if that were the case, we would go down to the Canadian Air Force Station at Sydney, Nova Scotia.

"Is Sydney on protected water?" he asked, and not knowing what he meant, I replied "Yes."

"Well, if it is on protected water, it is probably frozen solid and if it is, then what will you do?"

I answered to the effect that if Sydney were frozen over we would know about it before leaving Preswick and in such a case, in all probability we would have taken the southern route — the Azores to Belem or Natal, thence to Trinidad, Miami, and on to Washington.

"I have been told that a seaplane can land in the Azores waters only once in every ten or fifteen days. What will you do if you cannot land in the Azores?"

His questions were getting more pointed and to my mind, ruder, but I said that if this were the case, we would return to Lisbon or England because our fuel limitations would not permit us to proceed to South America.

"If you go to Lisbon," he hammered away, "all of you, I suppose, have civilian clothes?"

I answered, "Yes, all except General Marshall."

Churchill then inserted a knife: "I suppose you would like to see General Marshall interned?"

My response to this crack was simply to say that between all of us, crew and passengers, I thought we could outfit General Marshall in civilian clothes.

The PM got nasty, blurting out, "Young man, I don't think you know much about the job you are supposed to be doing, and I want you to know that I am holding you personally responsible for the safety of what I consider three of the most important people in our war effort!"

I inquired, "*Three* most important people?"

"Yes," Churchill shot back, "General Marshall, Harry Hopkins, and my First Sea Lord, Sir Dudley Pound."

This was the first I learned that Sir Dudley Pound would accompany us back to the United States. But whatever the case, I did not like the statement the PM had made about me so I said, "Sir, may I be excused?"

"Yes, and the best of luck to you," he ended the confrontation.

XXVI

1942: With Ike to England

I WENT BACK to Claridge's, where the MODICUM party waited for me. We made a speedy trip out to Croyden, and when we had our altitude, Wedemeyer, who sat next to me, asked me where our next stop would be. I answered, "Preswick, of course." He gave me a funny look, and the next time I looked out the window, we were over the Irish Sea headed for Ireland. We landed near Belfast, Harry Hopkins went off with the Governor General for lunch, Al disappeared with some friends, I was left with General Marshall and the Division Commander of our only ground forces in the British Isles. We three got into a car and drove out to the place where the Division passed in review — pretty strong medicine for me, as I had never seen a Division review before, and it is spectacular. After the review, we had lunch with the Division Commander and then went back to the Airfield.

"Where now, Howard?" Wedermeyer asked.

I replied, "Preswick."

This time he said, "No, Stranraer," a place I had never heard of. It was a Coastal Command Station of the R.A.F. in the southern part of Scotland, directly across the Irish Sea from Belfast.

Sure enough, we landed at Stranraer, and I was beginning to wonder who really had responsibility for the flight planning of MODICUM. Not a soul appeared on the airfield nor along the road to the lovely little hotel where we were escorted by our R.A.F. Officers. There were no other guests in the hotel. Harry Hopkins wanted to talk by phone to the President and one of the R.A.F. Officers instructed him in the use of the "scramble." When he had completed his call, General Marshall phoned General Eisenhower, his Deputy in the War Department.

Al and I thought both Hopkins and Marshall too optimistic in their reports. With our clipper at the pier and Sir Dudley Pound already aboard, we were ready for the flight back home, heading out of the harbor to the open sea in a pitch black sky. After we had gained our altitude and leveled off, I went up to the flight deck, told the two captains of the experience I had had with the Prime Minister and asked them to please let me know where we were headed. Captain Gray said, "New York. We have a fine tail wind and can make it nicely." This was news because over the North Atlantic the winds are usually westerly and sometimes very strong. This route, incidentally, was the one alternative I failed to tell the Prime Minister.

The flight required about sixteen hours, but we picked up nearly five hours in a change of time and landed at the Pan American Terminal at approximately eight a.m. New York time. Sir Dudley Pound stayed in his bunk during the entire flight. The President had sent his *Sacred Cow* to LaGuardia to pick us up and take us to Washingtoon and as soon as we were on the ground in the Capitol, I called General Arnold and said I would like to come over to his quarters at Ft. Myer and tell him what had happened in London. He sent a car over for me and soon I was telling him my idea of the British reaction to *Bolero* and *Roundup*. I rather thought that he did not believe that the British would buy the plan in the first place, but when I told him how Eddie Aldrin and I had obtained the use of the Burtonwood R.A.F. field, he fairly exploded. He called Barney Giles, his Chief of Staff, and told him to order all his domestic Air Force Commanders to be in Washington by nine o'clock the next day. This order required many of them to fly all night.

At the meeting the next morning, Arnold told the commanders that I had just returned from England with General Marshall and Harry Hopkins, with the idea of selling the British our *Bolero* and *Roundup* Plans. But whether or not the British bought them, Craig had something more important to tell them about — a Service Command in England. Then he turned the floor over to me, something I did not expect but I proceeded to relate how Eddie Aldrin and I got the Burtonwood Depot from the British.

General Arnold then turned to Major General Walter H. "Tony" Frank and told him he would be in charge of our Service Command in England, with Burtonwood as Headquarters of the organization. He wanted Tony to leave the next morning. Tony protested this assignment bitterly, and I think he blamed me for it, but as it turned out, it became one of our wisest decisions.

UPON MY RETURN to my office in Washington I set up a meeting with my section chiefs to brief me on the current situation. These meetings continued for several days. In the meantime, affairs were humming and toward the middle of June, General Arnold called me down to his office and asked me if I had met General Dwight D. Eisenhower. When I told him I had not, he suggested that I go over to his office in the War Department General Staff. At that time, Eisenhower, General Marshall's Deputy Chief of Staff, was preparing to leave for England to become Commanding General of the American Ground and Air Forces. Arnold had recommended me to him for a job on his staff.

That afternoon I met Eisenhower and liked him the minute I saw him. He was considerate and soft-spoken as he explained to me his gathering a staff together. As I had been recommended to him by both General Arnold and General Hull, he asked if I would join him in the flight to England, saying he did not have a definite staff post in mind at the moment but certainly would find one. He asked me to keep all of our conversation confidential, and to be prepared to leave from Bolling Field in two days.

Col. Orville Anderson was the next senior in the Division, so on my return to the office I called him in and told him, under the pledge of secrecy, that I had been assigned to England with Eisenhower. He remarked that the job of Chief, Air War Plans Division, certainly made one vulnerable for a change, and that he hoped it would work for him. (It did. Two months later he came to England as an Operational Planner with General Spaatz and remained in the 8th Air Force Headquarters until the end of the war.)

My secretary, seeing me clean out my desk, wanted to know the reason. I told her I was being reassigned overseas and not to ask any more questions. On arriving home that evening, I told my wife pretty much the same thing, knowing she would understand. Her startled reaction to this was: "Your daughter is getting married in a week, the announcements and invitations have been mailed, and you are supposed to give her away at the wedding. What are we going to do?" The only answer to this problem was to get someone to take my place in the ceremony. War upset everyone's life — but we had no choices to make, only alternatives.

My wife and daughter drove me out to Bolling two days later, and while we were standing near the C-87 assigned to us, watching the baggage being loaded, Generals Eisenhower and Mark Clark walked up and greeted me. I introduced them to Evangeline and our bride-to-be and Jeanne immediately said, "You know you are taking my father away just before my wedding?" General Eisenhower, looking at my beautiful daughter, said with a twinkle in his eye that he would leave me behind. I told him not to mind, that they could find someone to take my place, and besides it was about time to get aboard the airplane. After rueful good-byes, we climbed aboard the aircraft and were soon on our way. Jeanne and Dr. C. M. Stanfill were married two days later.

General Eisenhower, an expert bridge player found no one else aboard who played so we had to settle down with gin rummy. After a fuel stop and a bite to eat in Newfoundland, we made it straight into London with fairly good weather, to be met at Croydon Airport by some of the British Chiefs of Staff Committee and our our own Army Mission people, before we were whisked to Claridge's Hotel. As mentioned before, we were put up in the same rooms that had been provided for the Marshall-Hopkins party.

Someone, I suppose our Mission people, had provided us with office space in a building on Grosvenor Square. Diagonally across the Square stood the American Embassy, and Admiral Harold R. Stark had the building next door which housed the Naval Mission.

In the evening, General Eisenhower discovered he had been invited to attend the meeting of the British Chiefs of Staff at ten o'clock the next day. He asked me to go along with him and in the car taking us to the meeting, asked about the arrangement of the room where the meeting was to be held, who conducted the meeting, who attended and the complete drill, as he called it. General James E. Cheney, Air Corps,

Chief of the Army Mission and Admiral Ghormeley, Chief of the Navy Mission were there, much to my surprise, because I did not think they attended any Chiefs of Staff meetings.

After being greeted and introduced by General Sir Alan Brooke, General Eisenhower made a few remarks dealing mainly with his plans for the near future. After this, the meeting adjourned and we went home.

Eisenhower became known as the Commanding General, European Theatre of Operations (ETO) USA, and as such took over the Army Mission. The Mission was abolished shortly after his arrival, the personnel being absorbed in his Headquarters and other commands such as the 8th Bomber Command. He appointed me as Assistant Chief of Staff, G - 3, Plans and Operations, and since the only troops there were Air units, my principal job became keeping General Eisenhower informed of air action and preparing for the arrival of the ground force troops: first, a place for them to stay, and next, a place where they could exercise and maneuver.

General Mark Clark had set up Ground Force Headquarters at Salisbury, and it was my job to get requirements from him and work them out in the best possible way with the British. Ground space was at a premium, and finding room for the units as they arrived became a serious problem. The 8th Air Force did most of this work for the newly arriving air units.

The following months we were engaged in planning for *Torch*, the invasion of North Africa.

XXVII

1942: Operation TORCH, Gibraltar, Algiers

⊛   IN AUGUST, 1942, I received a promotion to Brigadier General. About the middle of September, Brigadier General Lyman L. Lemnitzer was appointed Assistant Chief of Staff, G - 3 (Plans and Operations), and for the time being I became a Deputy Chief of Staff principally engaged in planning at Norfolk House representing the air interest for operation *Torch*, working under Bedell Smith. On October 7th, the former Air Section of AFHQ Staff was redesignated as the Air Staff, AFHQ, with Air Commodore Arthur Sanders, R.A.F., as Chief. I was designated his assistant. Our job was to coordinate all air planning and to advise the Commander-in-Chief on all air matters. We were designated the Assistant Chief of Staff for Air and the Deputy Assistant Chief of Staff for Air, AFHQ.

Brigadier General James H. Doolittle had been named to command the American Air units of the expedition, known as the 12th Air Force, and Air Marshal Sir William L. Welsh commanded the corresponding R.A.F. units. The two commanders were directly responsible to General Eisenhower for their operations.

AFHQ advance echelon moved from London to Gibraltar by November 5, 1942. General Bedell Smith, the Chief of Staff of Headquarters, ETOUSA (European Theater of Operations, U.S.A.), remained in London. Air Commodore Sanders went with the echelon to Gibraltar, and I remained in London.

On November 8, 1942 — D-day for *Torch*, the day of the invasion of North Africa with landings on the West Coast at Agadir and on the north coast at Oran and Casablanca — I was with General Bedell Smith, the Chief of Staff, reading the messages which were coming in from Gibraltar. He spied one in particular and said to me, "They are now putting in the first team." This message stated that Air Commodore Sanders had been taken ill and was being returned to London and that Craig was to proceed to Gibraltar immediately. This pleased me very much, and while Bedell was calling up the 8th Air Forces to find out when the next plane would leave for Gib, I went back to the Dorchester Hotel, where most of us lived, to pack up. Bedell found that a plane which would have a place for me would leave one of the London airdromes that evening for a field on Land's End. I could be ferried to Gibraltar the next morning.

On Gibraltar, I reported to General Eisenhower and found him much perturbed over the absence of reports from the Task Forces. The British had sent an airplane over to the Casablanca force, but it had been shot down. He asked me to go to Algiers to find out why Mark Clark had not reported, and Jimmy Doolittle arranged for a B-17 to take me to the North African city. The Commander of an armored unit in control of the airdrome in Algiers told me that the German JU-88's would come in just at dusk each evening and bomb the hangar line and hangars.

I decided that we would park our B-17 out on the far side of the airdrome. It seemed to me unlikely that the Germans would make a separate trip just to get the B-17 or detach any of their planes to bomb it, but that is exactly what happened. While I went into Algiers to see General Clark, the crew had its dinner and then made up the bunks in the plane to get some sleep. All of them were in bed, except one man who was watching the bomb raid from the open door when the plane was hit — a *direct* hit. The man in the door was blown out about fifty feet and knocked unconscious, the rest of the crew were killed instantly.

I had dinner with General Clark, who sent another message back to Gibraltar, asking for confirmation on its delivery. It seems that a faulty communications system lay behind the C-in-C's failure to hear from Clark.

When we went out to the airfield to see what damage the raid had done, I found that my B-17 had been destroyed and all but one of the crew killed. The fact shocked me too much for me to express my feelings. While I talked on the line to Colonel Elliott Roosevelt, the lone survivor of my B-17 came wandering up to us in a state of shock. I took the poor fellow to the dispensary which the British R.A.F. had established and asked the doctor to look after him. The next day I caught a C-47 returning to the Rock and took the crew survivor, still in pretty bad shape, back with me.

By the time I returned, Eisenhower was receiving messages regularly from General Clark, and messages were beginning to come in from the Western Task Force, indicating that a landing had been successfully made and affairs were well in hand.

A few days later General Eisenhower left Gibraltar for Algiers, taking me along with his party. He established his headquarters at the St. George Hotel, where the residents were still being vacated. I found where my Air Office was to be located and began to settle there; Doolittle established his 12th Air Force Headquarters in an oil company building nearby. During this time, most of us were living and messing at the St. George and I will never forget some of those breakfasts in the early days of our establishment: red wine (with water) and dry toast made from stale bread.

We were being bombed each night and sometimes during the day. I remember one evening, when Colonel Allard of Doolittle's staff and I were talking to Doolittle in his room at the St. George, the Germans evidently tried to hit the Hotel. Several bombs came uncomfortably close, and the old building rocked on its foundations. I finally took a breather out in the garden; Colonel Allard joined with me, but Jimmy stuck it out. Fortunately, the place was not hit.

These bombing raids continued for weeks until finally Ike got weary of them and called a meeting one evening of Doolittle, Air Marshal William Welsh, Bedell Smith, Brigadier John Whitely of the British Army and me. Welsh's Headquarters were located several miles out of town, and while he was driving in, the Germans bombed the area, tearing up the only paved road. He had to make a detour, which caused him to be late for the meeting, irritating Eisenhower quite a bit.

"Freddie" Welsh, like most of the senior British Officers with whom I came in contact, had a gift of expressing himself clearly and distinctly. His very articulate explanation of the cause of the delay gave Ike a chance to calm down, and when Freddie finished we got on with the meeting. Ike explained his feelings about the continual bombings and wanted to know if anything could be done about it. Welsh explained that all his radar equipment, necessary for night fighting, had been buried in the bottom of the holds of the supply ships, as yet unloaded. He had already asked the Air Ministry for duplicate equipment but believed he would have his own out of the ships before he could get supplied from England. Doolittle said that he could only fight in the day time, and at that, he would have to have warning of an impending raid. After more discussion Eisenhower finally got around to me. I suggested that he ask "Tooey" Spaatz and Arthur Tedder to come to Algiers for consultation. They both had been fighting the German Air Force and maybe they would have some ideas of what to do. At the time, I did not realize how this would sound to Doolittle and Welsh, but it was no sooner out of my mouth than I wished I had not said it. Definitely it sounded like a reflection on the abilities of these two fine and able men, which of course I had not intended. Eisenhower said nothing, but the next day he asked both Spaatz and Tedder to come to Algiers.

XXVIII

1942: Command in Tunisia

WITHIN A SHORT TIME Spaatz and Tedder arrived in Algiers and went into a huddle with Doolittle and Welsh, coming up with a plan to reorganize our air arm into the Northwest African Air Forces. After a short visit in London, Spaatz came back to Algiers to stay. I returned to Cairo with Tedder in a B-17 and stayed at his house for a few days, visiting the Middle East Headquarters and meeting many of the senior people located there. Then Tedder sent me up to the Desert Air Force at Marble Arch to meet Air Marshal Sir Arthur Coningham. Coningham that evening took me over to Field Marshal Montgomery's mess, where we had a good meal. Montgomery asked many questions about General Sir Kenneth Anderson's Army in Tunisia and how affairs were going with it. The next day Coningham showed me how his air force operated with Montgomery's army, teamwork which I thought excellent, and it proved to be so. The next day I returned to Cairo to find that my plane had to have an engine change but finally another B-17, on its way back to the States from India, was ready, and I climbed aboard that one.

On this flight good weather prevailed until we passed Tripoli, then the clouds began to come in. I told the crew to climb above them because we would soon be running into the mountains of Tunisia and Algeria, and over the sea we would be a sitting duck for the German fighters based in Sicily. After some hectic navigating, all of us heaved a sigh of relief as we turned the plane toward the shore of Algeria. In a short time, through a rain shower, we spotted Algiers and then the runways at Maison Blanche. I told the crew where to put up while they were in Algiers, thanked them and wished them good luck on the remainder of their trip home.

A few days after General Spaatz returned to Algiers, he came over to my office and asked me if I would like to have command of the 12th Air Support Command in Tunisia. It consisted of a P-38 Group stationed at Youks-le-Bains and a P-40 Group at Thelepte. Their job was to support the American and French Ground Forces fighting in the area. Colonel Tommy Blackburn had command of the outfit at the moment, but had become ill and had to be relieved. I told General Spaatz I would like to have the job, and he said, "It is yours." The next day my orders were issued and I took off for Tunisia.

The Headquarters of the Command were located in the town of Tebessa, in a rather large frame building. This Headquarters had been a National Guard Observation Group HQ back in the States, redesignated as an Air Support Command when it arrived in North Africa. There had been no change in the internal organization and it seemed to me principally involved in paper work. Outside of routine matters, none of the officers seem to know what they were supposed to do.

Tommy Blackburn was in terrible shape with a double hernia, scarcely able to get out of bed. I had the doctor from Youks-le-Bains take a look at him, and he was horrified. He said Tommy would have to be taken to a hospital right away. Before we got a C-47 and put Tommy aboard, he turned over to me $10,000 in gold French coin, for which I gave him a receipt.

I next visited the Fighter Group at Youks-le-Bains and received what I considered a pretty cool reception. After lunch, I talked to the Group Commander and he appeared to me to be pretty much whipped down. He had been having a hard time with the Germans, losing many crews and P-38s with no replacements. He did not know how much longer he could hold out. When I returned to my headquarters, I sent a message to General Doolittle, recommending that the P-38 Group be withdrawn from combat and another fighter group, preferably the Spitfire Group he had back near Oran, be sent up to me. Orders were received shortly sending the P-38 Group back to Casablanca but informing me the Spitfire Group could not be spared. General Patton over in Casablanca had an apprehension about the Germans coming down through Spain and crossing over to Africa. With this theory, he tied up large forces, both land and air, for months.

However, Jimmy did send me a newly arrived P-39 Group, which I hid in a grove of trees near Thelepte, until we could warn and educate our own troops and the French about this new type of airplane.

The next day, I went over to see the P-40s at Thelepte. This group was commanded by Colonel John R. Alison with Colonel Phil Cochran as his Number 2 man. In fact, it seemed to me that both of these men were commanding the Group, and it was a fantastic outfit. Four or five men would dig a place in the ground, put a revetment around it, and sleep and eat in this bunker, cooking their meals there. The only office I could discover was an operations dug-out. The Group, however, was a first-class fighting outfit. I had known both Alison and Cochran at Langley Field when they were in the 8th Pursuit Group before the war. Later both of them were to distinguish themselves in Burma.

I asked them why the unusual field layout, and Alison answered by saying, "Stay over until tonight and we will show you." I accepted. I also asked them about their plan of operations, who ordered the flights, when, to where and for what. They replied that they did not get any orders to do anything. Once in a while Joe Cannon would ask them to escort his bomber formations, but that was about all. I stayed around the airfield the rest of the day, and finally Johnny Alison asked me in to his place for "dinner." He and Cochran had opened some cans, warming up the contents in an old frying pan over a small fire inside of the dugout, and we ate. It was very good, too. Just at dusk, we went outside, and Alison told me to watch over the mountains to the east. Soon a squadron of JU-88s came flying over the mountain top at low level and opened up machinegun fire on all the aircraft, putting several out of commission. I asked Alison why he did not put a "CAP" (a security flight of friendly aircraft) over the field about this time, and he said they could not afford to use up the gasoline. I then suggested that he have a squadron ready to take off as soon as the Germans were seen over the mountain, and go up and engage them. He said this sounded all right, and he would try it out the next night. I promised to be there.

When I drove over to Thelepte late the next afternoon, Alison was all set for the enemy planes. As soon as they were seen over the mountain, the squadron took off in all directions and went after the JU-88s. It turned out to be a regular turkey shoot with the Germans the turkeys — only one or two of them getting away. The German squadron commander was shot down and taken to a French hospital near where he fell. I got a telephone call from the French doctor at the hospital asking me to come over. When I arrived there, the place was in the utmost confusion. They had the German on the operating table working on him, while another group of doctors and orderlies were trying to keep the door closed on the American photographer Margaret Bourke-White who wanted to get in the room and take pictures of the operation. She told me she had General Spaatz's permission to be up there, and I had nothing to do with it. I told her to get out of the hospital and out of Tunisia and that my driver would take her back to Constantine. Eventually she got in the car and was on her way. The doctor in charge thanked me but I learned later the German airman had died. He was a veteran of World War I, a fine looking man, dressed in his uniform jacket and all his medals. He must have had a premonition that this would be his last mission and dressed for it.

Another incident about this raid concerned a youngster named Daniel Boone, flying his first combat mission with the American Squadron. At his debriefing, he said he thought he had shot down three Germans but did not know the location of them. In checking, Alison got a confirmation from our ground units who were watching the fight that one of our airplanes had shot down three E.A. (enemy aircraft) so he gave Boone credit for them. A few days later, Boone was shot down and killed in a fight with German FW-190s. I had recommended him for the D.S.C., which I think was given to his parents posthumously.

We had no more air raids on Thelepte.

XXIX

1942: Missions From Thelepte, Youks-les-Bains

⊛ SUPPLIES FOR MY TWO FIGHTER GROUPS were received over a single-track railroad that ended in Tebessa, but there seemed to be no regular schedule on which the train ran. I asked General Spaatz to send down a railroad expert to iron out these problems. This man soon arrived and said that the tonnage carried could be increased if some bridges up the line were rebuilt. I asked him how long this would take, and he estimated two weeks. Gasoline and oil were the items in greatest demand, and I thought if we could stock up on these two items, we would be able to span the delay.

However, two weeks went by with no trains and I ran out of gasoline. Further, I could not get any information when the train would start running again. I finally called Hamp Atkinson, who had a heavy bomber group at Biskra, about 150 miles southwest of Tebessa, to find out if he had a surplus of gasoline. He had and with the help of a French anti-aircraft officer who had recently arrived, I hired a camel train to bring drums of gasoline up from Biskra. The railroad train came in a few days later with plenty of gasoline, and I forgot about my camel caravan until late one night I heard a terrific roar in front of my house: There was the camel train, each animal with a fifty-gallon drum strapped on his back. With the help of my French Officer, I paid the fellow in charge of the camels with some of the gold coin I had. Fortunately the new capacity of the railroad proved ample for all our needs.

The P-39 group got off on its first mission about this time and had only one plane shot down, by our own anti-aircraft. I had them return to Youks-les-Bains, which had been vacated by the P-38 group, and here they stayed for the remainder of the war in Africa. The P-39 was completely outclassed by all German fighters in speed, climb and turning radius. I used this group only when the chance of being attacked was remote.

Colonel John K. "Joe" Cannon was a wonderful man with long experience as Director of Flying in the Training command. A fighter pilot, Cannon had spent almost all of his service in fighter units, but here he commanded bombers and did a good job of it. Ironically, all my service had been with bombers, and here I commanded the fighter units of the 12th Air Force. Joe had a house in Constantine and at Christmas time he invited me up to have dinner with him. General Spaatz also had a house there plus the advance echelon of his Headquarters. This visit with Joe was a real treat, a welcome break, for I had served with him in Hawaii and Randolph Field. Several long, long talks about our jobs and the Germans were very good for me. On Christmas Day, I went to church with George MacDonald, Spaatz's A-2 (Air Intelligence) and also a Philadelphian, and then back to Joe's place for dinner, an excellent turkey meal with all the trimmings, even a bottle of very good wine. While in Constantine, I learned about the Christmas Eve assassination of Admiral Jean Darlan. Admiral Darlan had been in charge of all the French forces in North Africa — given this command by the Nazi Commander of the German forces then occupying France. One time when I served on Eisenhower's staff, Darlan invited me to have lunch with him and his aides. I could never understand this invitation, except at the time Eisenhower and Bedell Smith were out of town and Darlan wanted to talk to some American. In any event, I was met at the gate of his villa by a French air officer and walked down a path, along which a squadron of native cavalry, all on white horses, were lined up wearing white bernousses and red sashes and caps and sitting at attention, as I walked by. I held a hand salute to them until we reached the house.

The luncheon was very pleasant. I do not believe Darlan ever got around to talk about the subject that bothered him but he was a very courteous person and easy to talk to through an interpreter.

Back in Tebessa, I found "Shorty" Hawkins, whom I had known at

Randolph Field, waiting for me. He had command of the Spitfire group at Oran, and said his people were getting restless, feeling that the war was passing them by. He said he would like to send up elements of about three planes, attach them to the P-40 group for a couple of days, and then return them home, when another element would come to Thelepte.

I told him that Doolittle and Spaatz would raise hell with both of us when they found out about it, and we would probably be fired from our jobs. Moreover, I would have to order the right sized ammunition for the Spitfire's British guns. This would bring up a question with the Ordnance supply people. "But let's try it out and see how it works," I said.

In a few days Alison had three Spitfires with his P-40 group and was perfectly delighted. As time went on, the little groups of three Spits grew to four, then six, then ten, and finally we were rotating by squadrons. The expenditure of Spitfire ammunition grew until finally the ordnance officer called me to ask what I was doing with all the British ammunition. I took him into my confidence about the Spitfires, telling him not to say anything to the 12th Air Force staff. But there were too many people involved, and one day Doolittle, himself in a Spitfire, flew into Thelepte, waited until the mission returned, saw the Spitfires, and asked Alison about it. He called me on the phone and told me to send them back and not to do that little trick again. I doubt if Spaatz or Patton ever heard about the incident, but it gave the boys in Hawkins' outfit something to talk about.

At this time, the French had what they called an Army Corps with its Headquarters located at Aire Bir. The General commanding this Corps asked me to come up and see him. He was a soft-spoken gentleman, white haired with a white mustache and had on a long white duster over his uniform. Through a translator, I learned he had one of his divisions boxed up in a canyon, and in every attempt to extract them, the German Air Force would clobber his troops. He wanted to know if I could furnish his division air cover while they escaped. I pointed out to him the importance of precision timing and speed, since the location of the trapped French division was under constant observation by either German aircraft or radar. I told him I would have to consult my fighter group commanders, to find out how best to conduct this operation.

The two group commanders and I decided we would work one squadron from each group at a time, the P-39s low the the P-40s high, that each squadron would stay over the division for two hours, and that they would start at eight o'clock the next morning. This would give the division six hours to get out of the canyon. I sent a message to the French General, outlining our proposal and urging speed on the part of the division. He agreed, and the exit from the canyon was made without incident the next day. A squadron of German fighters appeared but did not attack.

On another occasion, a small Army task force of ours shot down an ME-109 near Gafsa and captured the pilot, a non-commissioned officer who was very belligerent. The prisoner was delivered to Tebessa, where we had a huge POW cage, a large area enclosed with a barbed wire fence. I had a cot and mattress moved in, together with a bucket of water for washing, and left some canvas for him to make a cover over his cot.

We had just received a communications truck with all the latest equipment for intercepting enemy messages but the trouble was we had no one who could read German or speak German, so I sent a message off to Doolittle asking him to send me an interpreter. He arrived two days later, driving a car of his own and dressed in civilian clothes. This fellow was a Frenchman who had lived in Hamburg as a youth, later becoming an auto dealer in France.

I took him out to interrogate our prisoner. He had experience at this and started off very casually. Presently he got the German talking about his outfit and the new planes they were supposed to get and that sort of thing. The German said they were allowed to go out hunting alone, after so many missions, if they wanted to. He was on one of these hunting expeditions when he was shot down. Then something the Frenchman said indicated to the German that the interrogator was a Jew. The German spit on him and I had difficulty not cracking this "hunter" with a stick I carried. I arranged for him to be moved back to Constantine in an Army POW cage.

Through our intercept, we soon were able to get the German Air Force order of battle and the instructions issued to their units. We found out the German Air Force Headquarters was in Kairouan. The rule was not to act aggressively on any of these intercepts, otherwise the enemy would begin transmitting in codes, making everything more difficult. This radio truck boosted the morale of the communications section immeasurably, for they felt that now they were a part of the war.

Craig, Tedder, Wigglesworth, Timberlake in Algiers, 1943

XXX

1943: Mediterranean Air Command

✳ THE COMMANDING GENERAL of the Army Forces in Tunisia was Major General Lloyd R. Fredendall. Known as the II Corps, it had come over from Oran to New Headquarters in Constantine, where it had the job of covering the southern part of the line. At this time, when Air Marshal Welsh sent me down two Beau night fighters, we had a CAP flying over Tebessa, Youks and Thelepte, and when these two Beaus came sneaking in at almost ground level, they were promptly shot down by the CAP. The Beaus had Canadian crews aboard who were unharmed but madder than all get-out. I radioed Welsh what had happened, and he sent two more down the next day, giving us ample warning.

Rumors constantly circulated that the Germans were going to attack our Headquarters with parachute troops. One night I received a telephone call from General Fredendall's G-2, telling me that the Germans were going to drop some paratroopers at my Headquarters that night and I had better get my night fighters up. I told him we did not have the equipment for directing a night fighter on a target and that there was no sense in sending them up just to fly around in the dark. General Fredenall then got on the phone and told me to put those night fighters in the air — that he was not asking my advice but *ordering* me. I told him that if one of these planes had to come down and was captured by the enemy, it would compromise the entire air defense of Great Britain. He said he did not care about that, but as soon as those German transports with their paratroops came over my place, he wanted them shot down. And he hung up on me. I went over to the tent where the two Beau pilots were waiting and explained to them that this ground general, who was my boss, wanted them to get into the air and shoot down the German transports when they came over. I told them that I knew this was an impossible order, but I thought if they would just take off, circle the field and land, everybody would be happy. It had started to rain, which added to the dreariness of the affair. The pilots said O.K. and went out to their planes and took off. That was the last time I saw them. I waited around for about an hour but when neither returned, I went back to my office and phoned General Spaatz, relating what had happened. He said to be in his office at nine o'clock the next morning and we would go over to see General Fredendall.

They had a really heated discussion for about fifteen minutes, when in answer to a question by Spaatz, Fredendall said he thought I was doing a good job in Tebessa and wanted me to stay on. I never understood how he arrived at this opinion because the night fighter incident had been the first contact I had had with his headquarters.

The next day, when I returned to Tebessa I received a call from Air Marshal Welsh, asking how the night fighters were working out. I had to tell him about the night before, and he said he knew all about it. The two Beaus had flown up to their own airdrome at Bone and landed safely.

Shortly after the night fighter incident, the signal officer from II Corps came in to see me to explain that Corps Headquarters was moving down to the vicinity of Tebessa and would have to take over my telephone lines. I told him, "Nothing doing, put in your own lines as we had to do. I *have* to have phone communication with my two airdromes and 12th Air Force Headquarters in Constantine." Saying he was only carrying out orders, he left. I phoned Doolittle on this one, and he said he would see what he could do.

I began to feel physically run-down at this time, running a fever and spending time in bed away from my duties. Colonel Ed Lynn, the 12th Air Force Ordnance Officer, an old friend of mine, came down to Tebessa to see me. I lay in bed, and after taking one look at me, he sent for the doctor at Youks-les-Bains. The doctor diagnosed my trouble as double pneumonia and ordered a C-47 to take me back to the hospital at Algiers.

As soon as Doolittle heard about this, he sent Colonel Paul L. Williams from the Troop Carrier Command to relieve me. I took "P.L.," as we called him, over to meet General Fredendall, who had moved to a place near Tebessa. When I took P.L. over to the fighter group at Thelepte to meet the Group Commander, Alison remarked that Commanders of the Air Support Command seemed to be expendable. Vincent Sheean, the author and correspondent, then a lieutenant colonel in Doolittle's headquarters, accompanied me back to Algiers and entered me in the hospital.

In two weeks I was released as a convalescent. General Spaatz offered me a room in his pleasant house during this time, a lovely big house in the country which accommodated most of his immediate staff.

We were still having bomb raids on various sections of Algiers but mostly on the airdrome at Maison Blanche and the ships in the harbor. I remember going up on the roof of the Spaatz house one evening and watching a raid on the city.

Harold Willis and I had picked the house for General Spaatz some time before. The Allied French officers in Algiers had made a list of all known residents who had collaborated with the Germans, and their homes were requisitioned first. When we showed the man who owned the place our papers, he became very much upset. We tried to calm him down, and also his wife and daughter, long enough to have them show us the inside of the house, which was furnished very beautifully. There was a large carriage house near the front of the driveway, and we told the family they could move in there, taking all their personal belongings with them, but not moving any of the house furnishings. We would take good care of everything as we would only be there a couple of months. General Spaatz liked the place, and the first evening after he moved in, he invited the family to join us for an informal dinner. During the meal the Frenchman asked why we were not serving wine. Harold Willis said we did not have any, whereupon the Frenchman said, "Come with me," and took him down to the basement, one part of which served as a wine cellar with hundreds of bottles of wine racked up in stands. He turned the key over to Willis and picked out two bottles of his choicest vintage which was excellent indeed. Affairs with the family were very cordial after this dinner, and by inviting the family General Spaatz showed once more his native genius and humanity. This home was a perfect place for a pneumonia convalescent, and daily I grew stronger.

About this time Eisenhower invited me to a big dinner party at his home. He had invited all the big wheels attending the Casablanca Conference (January 14-23, 1943) to come over to Algiers. After asking about my health, he asked me to act as his aide during the time these people were in Algiers, and of course I accepted. He said King George VI would attend the dinner he was planning to give, also PM Churchill plus the Joint and Combined Chiefs of Staff. He gave me a list of the people he expected to attend and suggested I get in touch with Bob Murphy, our State Department advisor, a really wonderful person, to prepare a seating arrangement. Bob and I sat down and started moving the names around like a checker game. Finally, we came up with a solution, except out of some sort of false modesty, I left my name off the list and so did Bob. General Eisenhower would have no part of this, saying we should keep our eyes on him for signals in the event something went wrong.

Late in the afternoon of the day of the party, I dressed in my best uniform and went to Ike's house to see how everything was progressing. I even checked with the butler, who was responsible for everything connected with the dinner. We went over the courses, the wine and dessert to be served. Everything seemed to be in order, so I asked the butler to bring me a scotch and soda, feeling I had a long tough evening ahead of me.

The house that General Eisenhower occupied was in a beautiful location, high upon a hill overlooking the Bay of Algiers. While I stood at the window, admiring the view, I heard a voice in back of me saying, "Young man, what are you holding in your hand?" I turned around to find Prime Minister Churchill, dressed in a tuxedo, looking at me very hard. I told him I had a scotch and soda, but that he could have anything he wished. He said, "I would like to have a brandy and soda." I pulled the cord and told the butler to bring the Prime Minister his drink. This over with, Churchill turned his attention to me. "I have seen you somewhere before," he said. "Don't tell me — let me guess." Then he asked me my name and that rang his bell. "Oh, you were the young man who came to England about a year ago with Harry Hopkins and General Marshall, and you didn't seem to know how you were going to get home."

I said, "Yes, Sir, that is one way of putting it, but I think you will remember we made a nonstop flight from Stranraer to New York City?"

He said, "Of course, I remember it, you had my first Sea Lord aboard, and I congratulate all who were responsible for the flight." I thanked him, although I believed he thought me a bit presumptuous. The guests started to arrive, and we had to bring our conversation to a close — probably a good thing for me.

After completing my social detour of duty, I returned to General Spaatz, who had plotted out almost entirely the new air organization called the Northwest African Air Force, virtually an all-American unit. Spaatz was waiting for Air Marshal Sir Arthur Tedder to arrive. Tedder was to become overall air commander of the Mediterranean from Gibraltar to Cairo, this organization to be known as the Mediterranean Air Command.

Soon Tedder landed, bringing with him some of his staff among whom was Pat Timberlake, a new US Air Corps B.G. At his first meeting with Spaatz, Tedder asked if he could have me as his chief of staff in the M.A.C. Pat was A-3, Operations. The other staff members were R.A.F. people. Tedder had as his Deputy Commander, Air Vice Marshal Wigglesworth, R.A.F., situated in the organization between Tedder and me. The British do not have a Chief of Staff in any of their military organizations, and for a while it appeared that either Wigglesworth or I would become a fifth wheel. However, after explaining to "Wiggy" that my job would be one of managing the staff and headquarters functions and doing such other jobs as the Chief wanted done, and that I understood Wiggy would be concerned principally with current operations and planning future operations, we finally got our work sorted out and affairs ran along rather smoothly.

Everyone on the M.A.C. staff seemed anxious to make it work. We all lived in a big comfortable home which the Air Chief Marshal called "Air House." We had our meals there, four days on British rations with British cooking and three days on American rations and American cooking. Our American ration was by far superior.

It was here I received a new Plymouth car which everyone seemed to borrow along with its driver, Sergeant Shindler.

Pat Timberlake and I liked to get up at a fairly early hour, have breakfast and get down to the office by eight o'clock. This gave me time to prepare for a Chiefs of Staff meeting at nine o'clock and the Commanders' meeting at ten. At the earlier meeting, we would recite the activities of the forces for the previous day and night. Spaatz had moved his Headquarters up to Constantine by this time, and I had a difficult time getting the staff to send down their activity report by wire. Often I would have to phone. Spaatz's HQ reluctance was due to their fear of interception by radio transmission or wire-taps on the phone. Commodore Dick of the Royal Navy and executive officer for Admiral Andrew B. Cunningham (C-in-C, Naval operations) at these meetings would perpetually ask me for information about what the Air Force was going to do that day. I had to tell him I did not know nor could I find out, but he continued his needling until one morning I exploded and told him to stop asking that question, that security would not permit its transmission. He ceased his questioning then, and afterward Bedell said to me, "I am glad you told that fellow off. I have been wondering how long you would be able to take it."

Walter Bedell "Beetle" Smith was a remarkable man. Although suffering from ulcers or some such alimentary trouble, he seldom missed a day of duty. Often when Ike was having trouble with his commanders, he would send Bedell Smith out to calm them down. Smith was particularly successful with Field Marshal Montgomery, who constantly stirred up difficulties. I liked Bedell Smith tremendously and admired him as a man and a soldier. After the war, he became our Ambassador to Russia and did very well with that difficult job, which required a rare blending of tact, diplomacy and toughness.

Shortly after I returned to duty in Mediterranean Air Command Headquarters, Spaatz asked me if I would like to pin the Air Medal on four of the pilots of the Lafayette Squadron which had served under me at Thelepte. When I agreed, he said, "Nine o'clock tomorrow at Maison Blanche Airdrome," (the principal airfield for Algiers).

The next day at Maison Blanche, Ted Curtiss, General Spaatz's Chief of Staff, met me and said that Brigadier General Everett Cook, Spaatz's

G-1, had the medals but had not yet arrived. So we walked out to the hangar line, where I met a French General who commanded a division lined up on the flying field. An American division was also present plus a bunch of women who were arranging refreshments in one of the hangars. We waited and waited for Cook and the medals. Finally, I suggested to the French General that we parade the troops, to which he agreed. This consumed another fifteen or twenty minutes, and still no Cook, no medals. Finally, Ted Curtiss with an armload of diplomas, each with a red ribbon around it, came out to the place where the French General and I stood impatiently. He said he did not have the medals but thought we could go on with the ceremony with these diplomas.

The recipients were called forward, and I congratulated each and handed out the diplomas. The honorees then stood alongside us while the troops marched by. At the conclusion of the parade, Ted Curtiss came to me and said, "We had better get out of here." When I asked him why, he said that the "diplomas" were blank pieces of paper which he had rolled up in the office while we were parading the troops. He found a car and we left. The next day the medals were delivered to the French aviators. A few years later, while on duty in Washington, I heard about this incident again.

In the late spring of '43 when the campaign in Tunisia drew to a close, I was told one morning that I would have to brief the commanders on the situation in Tunisia. I gathered up all the information I could think of and made my presentation. When I had finished, General Eisenhower asked about the air situation, and I proceeded, still omitting what Ike thought an important item: one of our pilots had shot down seven or eight German transports loaded with troops. This made quite an impression on my audience, but I explained that the reason I had failed to mention it was that this sort of thing had become routine with our people.

The war in Tunisia came to an end on May 7, 1943. A victory parade was held in Tunis on the 20th to mark the end of the Axis effort in Africa. I flew up to Tunis and found a place in the stand of the reviewing officers, with Ike and Montgomery. In the brilliant sun, I began perspiring all over in my winter uniform and soon felt dizzy from the sun beating down on my head. I thought I might have a recurrence of the sunstroke I had suffered in Hawaii many years before. Very soon a British Scots Division came marching by with their bagpipes playing full out. They were a handsome sight in their clean khaki uniforms, short-sleeved shirts and short trousers. Then came our poor old 34th Division, with full packs and anti-gas-treated wool uniforms, with no band and led by a boy who had once worked in my office in London. The contrast between the two units, British and American was terrific. In fact, the difference was so great, I felt I had to get out of the sun before I fainted and finally found a car which took me out to the airport, where I could get inside the building. Afterwards, General Eisenhower asked me what had happened. He had missed me at the Bey's luncheon, at which I was to receive some kind of medal.

A few days later I returned to Tunis with Harold Willis, looking for another house for General Spaatz. We finally found the house that Jurgen von Arnim the German Army Commander, had lived in and went up to see about it. This house was located on top of a hill, with beautiful landscaping and a view of the beaches and sea for miles. On a clear day we could see the Bon Peninsula easily.

On the street, as we waited for our jeep, another jeep with two MPs and a German officer drove up and stopped. One of the MPs said they had been authorized to bring the German out of the POW Cage so that he could surrender to an American Flying Officer. I said OK. The German got out of the jeep, very formally saluted us and said in German that he was the German Air Force Commander and he would surrender only to an American flying officer. He then offered me his sword. Willis, who understood what he was saying, interpreted for me. I took the sword in both hands and handed it back to the German, telling him to turn it in at the POW cage. He unfastened a ceremonial dirk, which was strapped to his belt, and offered that to me. I kept the dirk and have it to this day. When our jeep arrived, we returned to the flying field and proceeded on to Constantine, where we described the place to General Spaatz and told him we thought he would like it.

Below the house was a lovely beach. Later on Montgomery's Army camped along this beach, and about three o'clock in the afternoon the whole army went bathing stark naked, having a wonderful time. They had been doing this sort of thing clear across the top of Africa.

XXXI

1943 : Malta, Sicily, the Pentagon

WE WERE NOW ENGAGED in planning the attack on Sicily, but first it was decided to capture the island of Pantelleria, lying roughly between Sicily and the Northern Coast of Tunisia. It possessed an airfield from which Axis planes were able to operate against us, but more than this, we badly needed the airfield ourselves in order to furnish additional support for Sicilian attacks. The island defenses were manned by Italians who, we believed, had had all the fighting they wanted and who would be looking for an excuse to quit. In a period of six days nearly 5,000 tons of high explosive bombs were dropped on the eastern end of the island. The garrison surrendered as our troops were boarding their assault boats.

Malta was yet another important island for the fighters who would engage in the assault on Sicily. From Malta a constant bombardment of sensitive points in Sicily was kept up to maintain control of the air. The assault of Sicily was to be made on the night of July 10, 1943, and I made a flight to Malta where Air Marshal Parks commanded the island's air forces. He wanted to know what I had in mind and I told him I would like to go to Gela, Sicily, as soon as he had word that the place was safe for a landing. A clearance came through the next day, July 11. He put me aboard a small two-engine transport and landed me there with a squadron of fighters for cover. General George Patton was at the airfield, and when I met him, he wanted to know who and where the VIPs were. When I told him I was the VIP, he turned away with a look of disgust but asked me to come up to his CP and see how the war was going. Everything looked very good. Maj. Gen. Lucien Truscott, Jr., a classmate of mine at Fort Leavenworth, was making remarkable progress with his Third Division on the eastern end of the island, and Montgomery seemed to be doing well on his way up from Syracuse toward Catania. Another plane which landed with some passengers for Gela was returning to Algiers, and I thumbed a ride in it.

I stopped in my office for a few minutes, and Wigglesworth told me that the Chief was considering moving his Headquarters up to Tunisia or to Malta, depending on where AFHQ would go. He said there was not much to be done about it now, except to figure out the space we would need. Spaatz had moved his headquarters to Tunisia, and the communications with it were still poor. And Bedell Smith wanted to see me as soon as I came in.

Bedell said that orders had been received to send me back to Washington for duty. Although Ike had sent a personal message to General Arnold asking him to reconsider these orders, a reply had come in from Arnold explaining I had been the first one sent out of Army Headquarters, and there were others waiting to go; besides he said, he needed me very much on his staff. I went back to Wigglesworth and told him of my disappointment in leaving the Headquarters. An Air Corps B.G., Gordon Saville, was being sent over to replace me. Wiggy said how sorry they would be to lose me.

When Eisenhower returned to Algiers, we had a little ceremony out in the garden of the St. George. Ike pinned the Legion of Merit medal on me in the presence of General John Whitely, Commander Harry Butcher and Bedell Smith, said a few nice words to me and bade me good-bye. That afternoon I caught a C-47 for Marakech, Morocco, from there I had a ride in a C-54 to London, where I remained several days awaiting a plane home.

At the Air Transport Command Office in London, I met Frank Brady, who was also returning home. We had a pleasant flight back to Washington. I got a car at Bolling which carried me out to my home in Silver Springs, and I burst into the house as a surprise to my family. It was a great reunion!

The next morning I went down to the Pentagon to check in with General Arnold. He wanted to know all about the British fleet's firing on our transports and gliders carrying paratroopers into Sicily. I was made Chairman of a special board to investigate this incident. We found the fleet commander partially at fault and the remaining responsibility for the incident due to communications people not requesting a confirmation of the messages that had been sent postponing the operation for one day. General Arnold was very unhappy about this affair.

From Barney Giles, Arnold's Chief of Staff, I took over the OC&R (Operations, Commitments & Requirements) Division, a tough job and an office that served as a receptacle for new problems thrown out by General Arnold. Early in my association with OC&R I discovered, in the Air Defense Section a young, baldheaded colonel named William McKee, nonrated, serving as executive officer of the section. I brought this Air Defense man up to the front office to take the place of my executive who departed, and count it as among my smartest moves. McKee was a jewel, capable, reliable. Later on he won the confidence of General Arnold and Secretary Stuart Symington and his talents were recognized in his rapid promotion to four-star general.

In August I received my own promotion to Major General, which carried with it a new responsibility. Arnold, taking a little time away from his desk on Sundays, appointed one of his staff MGs to take his desk, answer calls and act on anything needing immediate action. My first Sunday on this job threw me into the midst of a very interesting problem.

A Courier Messenger with a locked case came in and since I had been instructed to open all messages except those specifically marked for Arnold's eyes only, I read a Top Secret communication from General George Brett in Australia which said that twelve airplanes had been received there from the Navy and were looking good except for the absence of solenoids (a type of switch) for the planes' forward guns. Brett said he had checked all over Australia and could not locate similar solenoids or even a place that could manufacture them and he wanted General Arnold to ship him the urgently needed pieces of equipment.

Working first with Maj. Gen. Oliver Echols, our Director of Materiel, we determined the type of airplane the Navy had in Australia, then located a factory in New Jersey which fabricated the switches. Echols told them to put 100 of the solenoids in a bag and we would send for them.

The problem then centered on how to get the solenoids out to Brett in Australia. At this time, the Pacific was closed to all aircraft traveling to Australia from Hawaii and the only way I could see to fly the parts was via the South Atlantic to Africa, across Africa to the Indian Ocean, then to the Malay Peninsula and on to Australia. Echols responded that it was a hell of a long trip for a bagful of solenoids.

I took responsibility for chartering a Pan-American clipper to take this priority cargo to Brett in Australia. At lunch time I met General Tom Handy, Marshall's assistant, who asked me if I had any news. knowing he had seen the message from Brett, I told him the whole story of locating the solenoids and shipping them out by chartered plane. "Boy, Craig," Handy said with a grin, "you have a nerve chartering that clipper for such a voyage. I hope you don't have to pay for it!"

Later on I learned that when Handy returned to his office, Secretary Stimson came in to say he had a luncheon engagement with the President and did Tom have any war news the President might be interested in. Tom said "No, sir. I did just have lunch with Howard Craig and he has chartered a Pan-American Clipper plane to fly some solenoids over to General Brett in Australia. The plane will have to go via the South Atlantic and the Indian Ocean." Stimson, who must have been a trifle confused at this narrative to begin with, just said that was fine.

The next I heard of this affair was a phone call from General Arnold who wanted to know what in hell was going on. He said the President had just called to congratulate him on getting a Pan Am Clipper to haul a load of hemorrhoids to Brett via the South Atlantic and Indian Oceans!

XXXII

1944-45: Theaters of War, An Incident with Patton

WE WERE BEGINNING to have trouble on replacement crews and airplanes. Most of the heavy bombers were flown over my North Atlantic route to England or over the South Atlantic route to Italy by their replacement crews, but extra crews were needed to replace those completing their required fifty missions and being sent home.

Colonel McKee secured for me from the Harvard Graduate School of Business Administration a Dr. Edmund Learned and his assistant, Myles Mace, to try to solve the problem of where the replacement crews and planes were being lost. In the meantime, I had taken steps of my own. Forbes Air Force Base in Kansas served as the clearing center for all crews and planes on their way overseas. I sent one of my young men out to Forbes with a letter explaining his presence to the Commanding Officer, asking that he be put in a replacement crew going to Italy. This fellow had a fantastic experience, finally winding up in a ground forces replacement camp near Oran, along with hundreds of other crew replacements. I wired Ira Eaker to break the crews loose from the camp. With General Spaatz and his fighter airplane replacements, it was just a story of poor arithmetic and carelessness in handling the records. Dr. Learned, however, installed a system which eliminated all further trouble.

Came a day toward the end of the war in Europe when Dr. Learned entered my office with a complicated chart which showed the production and loss rate of our B-17s and B-24s. Amazingly, the chart demonstrated that while our losses were rapidly decreasing, production of these aircraft rolled along at the same rate. Clearly, if we did not slow down or even stop production, we would soon be looking for places to store these new planes. I questioned Learned thoroughly on this fantastic situation but he had the answers and "back up" to those answers.

I made an appointment for the two of us to see Arnold that afternoon and the General, as surprised as I was, said he wanted Learned to make this same presentation to General Marshall. Marshall in turn wanted Secretary Stimson to see it, and Stimson asked only one question, "Does this mean we will start closing down our aircraft manufacturing plants?" When given a positive answer, he said we would have to tell President Roosevelt about it. Afterwards the President made the public announcement that production at certain aircraft plants would be slowed down or even discontinued. By this one piece of solid research Dr. Learned saved the government millions of dollars.

One morning about a month after Dr. Learned's bombshell, General Arnold told me that I was being transferred to the War Department General Staff as Ed Hull's deputy. My first reaction was that I did not like the idea of being separated from the Air Corps again but Arnold said, "You will probably be able to do more for the Air Corps in that position than any job you might have over here. You might like to know that Ed Hull asked for you, and he had the choice of any officer in the Army." That made me feel much better. I liked and admired Ed Hull tremendously, as a man and as a soldier.

Hull outlined my duties: I would take over the Theater Section which handled all the Theaters of the War but now that the War in Europe was ending, my principal concern would be the Pacific. He mentioned that one of the big problems would be the movement of troops from Europe to the Pacific. Some of them would travel by transport from Europe and through the Panama Canal to their assignments in the Pacific; others would spend a short leave of absence in the States, then reembark for the Pacific. Still others who had long combat records would be held in the United States as a Reserve.

I asked that Johnny Barker, then with Eaker in Italy, be assigned to me. Johnny, a classmate at Leavenworth and one of the most unflappable people I ever met, did a wonderful job in these months in scheduling the European divisions to their various destinations.

One of the duties I inherited with the Theater Section took me along with VIPs on their trips to Europe and later to Japan. I made several trips with Marshall; I remember one in particular, just before the end of the war in Europe.

General Marshall and I had gone pretty far up in the front lines when we saw the men of a division resting alongside of the road. Marshall stopped the car, talking and questioning the men as we walked along. Soon we met the Division Commander, Major General Norman Cota, my old Finance Officer friend at Langley Field back in the 20s. He said they had just got out of contact with the Germans and had been in the line for ten tough days, and were very tired. But after a short rest he was sure they would be ready to go back in again. Marshall asked him what division he had, and Cota just stared blankly at him. I finally said the 28th Division, and Cota came back to earth to say, "Yes, the 28th." He added, "I'm sorry, General, but I am so tired I just couldn't think for a minute." General Marshall said he understood very well.

I made one trip to Paris with Governor James F. Byrnes, the Director of War Mobilization, General Marshall, and General Tom Handy in the President's *Sacred Cow*. The plane, piloted by Lieutenant Colonel Henry T. "Hank" Myers, had flown nonstop from Newfoundland, the first publicized flight direct to Paris. Generals Marshall and Handy stayed at Eisenhower's place in Rheims, and Governor Byrnes, a wonderful companion, and I were put up in a lovely house known as Brown House, in Paris.

On another visit to Europe, with Mr. John J. McCloy, then Assistant Secretary of War, we got down to Frankfurt where General Patton had his headquarters. We had dinner with the General and his people found a place for us to stay the night. The next morning, a Sunday, Mr. McCloy told Patton he would like to visit the head of the U.S. Military Government in Frankfurt. Patton got two tanks warmed up with McCloy and Patton's aide in the leading tank; Patton and I were in the one following. We started off with a roar and clatter, and the first thing we knew we were lost. The Military Government Headquarters Chief was a Regular Army Lieutenant Colonel located in the I.G. Farben Building in the middle of the city, and finally, after much changing of routes, we made it to this building, all along the wall of which for several blocks, stood a queue of people waiting to get into the Headquarters for licenses, permissions, and similar official paperwork. Getting out of the tank, Patton called to one of the Military Policemen keeping order in the line, and asked him if he spoke German. The MP said he did so Patton told him to tell all the women in the line to bend their knee as he went by and all the men to remove their caps and hats. I thought this pretty strange and funny and started to laugh, but Patton was serious about it — and the knee bending and hat doffing continued as we went up the line to the door where McCloy and the aide were waiting.

We went up the stairs of the Office of Military Government, where the Chief introduced himself to McCloy. He said he had come into Frankfurt with the "point" of the Third Army several days before and had appointed a mayor, was in the process of getting a city council together, had restored electricity and water to the city, was now checking the sewers to see that they were working, had reestablished the police and fire department, and had published regulations for the people of the occupied city.

Patton asked the Chief if he needed anything, and the Military Government officer said he did but had already requisitioned his needs through his own channels. Patton questioned him closely about that saying, "You belong to the Third Army, and I do not see why you don't call on the Third Army when you need help." The Chief of the Mission said he did not belong to the Third Army and received his orders and instructions directly from the Secretary of War. Mr. McCloy stepped in at this point and said it was true, all of the Officers of Military Government operated directly under the Secretary of War, particularly his own office, and if General Patton would now excuse him, he wanted to talk to this Military Government Officer alone. So a defeated Patton said, "Come along, Craig, we will meet them down below."

Downstairs Patton stormed around. Finally, he came up to me and said, "What did you think of that fellow upstairs?" I said I thought he had done a pretty good job. "Good, hell!" Patton exploded. "He is nothing but a goddamned windbag!"

About that time McCloy came down and we all returned to Patton's Headquarters. When we arrived there, Patton said to me, "These other people have something else to do. Would you like to come with me to visit a field hospital?" I told him I would like very much to go, so off we went, this time in a jeep. The hospital was located a short distance outside of Frankfort and we walked right into the operating room of a large tent where doctors were operating on a man who had been shot in the stomach. Soon the principal surgeon took Patton by the arm and escorted him outside saying that the man would be all right but that there would have to be some rearrangement of his plumbing before he could be up and about again. I later learned the wounded man was Patton's son-in-law.

XXXIII

1945: MacArthur; With Ike to Peking

BACK IN WASHINGTON, upon my reporting to Marshall,
I learned the Secretary of War had just received a message to
the effect that the House and Senate would have a joint meeting at ten o'clock the next morning and that they wanted a report on
the state of the war. Secretary Stimson was to arrange it, and he had
designated General Marshall to give the Army and Air Corps side of
the report and Admiral Ernest J. King the Navy side. He wanted me
to write up the text of his report in conjunction with Brigadier General
Thomas North of our Current Affairs Branch and to have it ready by
8:30 in the morning. He wanted me to start on the West Coast of the
United States and move easterly across the country, mentioning our
major ground and air activities, where new divisions and air squadrons
were being formed, and our rate of shipments from the east coast to
England. Then I should pick up the situation in England and France,
the number of divisions and air groups we had engaged, move over to
Italy and give the same information there, then to the Middle East,
India, the Hump, China, the number of squadrons fighting the Japanese, then to MacArthur's forces, our heavy bombers on Saipan and
Tinian and what they were doing, then to Hawaii and Alaska, and back
to the West Coast.

I got in touch with General North of the Current Branch and told
him to hold his men at the office and to come and see me right away.
North and his men and I managed to complete the final draft about
five A.M. and at 8:30 I waited for General Marshall to call me into
his office from the anteroom. Whenever any of us presented a draft

of a paper to Marshall, his first action was to pick up his pen to edit and make corrections. This time he held his pen high, ready to jump on any mistakes, and went through page after page without making a mark. Finally he finished with the paper and said it was fine. Back in my office, I briefed General Hull on the situation, then phoned North and told him the paper appeared to be all right.

When we arrived at the auditorium of the Library of Congress, I pinned a world map on a stand. Marshall placed our paper on the podium; then Secretary Stimson arrived, and I took a seat in the last row of seats. In a few minutes, Stimson explained that General Marshall and Admiral King would give the briefing.

Marshall started off, without referring directly to the paper but reciting from it almost word for word, and he covered the entire world without a break. When he finished, the audience rose and gave him a standing ovation.

Admiral King lowered his head over the podium and as he read his paper, and a couple of young officers were changing maps for him, but soon they got out of sequence with the text of the talk, and it became impossible to understand what the Admiral was talking about. Representative Clare Booth Luce slid into a seat beside me and said, "Isn't it awful?" I asked her how she liked General Marshall and she said, "He was magnificent. He should be an actor." Finally, Mrs. Luce said she could take it no longer and left.

When Admiral King finished, I went back to the stage to recover my map and the speech paper, but Marshall had both of them, and we left for the Pentagon.

On the way back Marshall asked me, "How did it go?" I told him that he was at his very best and that the ovation he received indicated that the Congressmen and Senators liked it. I told him of the incident with Clare Luce, which greatly amused him. It was without a doubt one of the finest demonstrations of its kind that I had ever witnessed. The man, I know, had read our paper through only once, and yet he recited it word for word for thirty or forty-five minutes. General Marshall, from that day, became to me a giant of a man, with an intellect to match.

TOWARD THE END OF 1945, shortly after General Eisenhower became Chief of Staff of the Army, he decided to go to Peking to see the war in the Pacific and to visit General Marshall, then in Peking as a consultant to Chiang Kai-shek. Our first stop in Hawaii was a social whirl for him; our next was for gas at Iwo Jima, where we were met by a sunburned Colonel Chil Wheeler of the Air Corps.

We landed in a drizzling rain in Tokyo to be met by General Douglas MacArthur and his staff at the airport. It amazed me that General MacArthur had recognized me as I came down the gangplank, and greeted me by name. On my former visit to his headquarters at Tacloban on the island of Leyte, just prior to the fall of Manila, with the Richardson Board that was obtaining the views of our senior commanders on the organization of a Department of Defense after the war, I had seen General MacArthur only for a few minutes. A dinner at MacArthur's house was held that night, and the next day we were off to Peking.

We arrived in Peking in midmorning, and after pleasantries with the greeting party, the Generalissimo and Madame Chaing had us to lunch. I was very happy to see General Marshall looking so well; I think I was the only member of Ike's party invited to this luncheon.

From Tokyo we returned via Guam and Hilo, Hawaii. After we left Guam, Eisenhower asked me if there was not some place we could go for a few days' rest, rather than back to the social whirl of Honolulu. I mentioned Hilo on the Island of Hawaii, as I understood the Army had a very nice R & R Camp at the Volcano. I was sure we could arrange to have the hundred-hour inspection of the airplane done there and receive adequate weather reports and a clearance to San Francisco. He said, "Tell the pilot we are stopping at Hilo. We are not going to Honolulu."

I sent wires to Hickam, requesting the services at Hilo, and everything was perfectly arranged. I also sent a message to the manager of the airport at Hilo, asking him to give no publicity to General Eisenhower's presence. Ike was delighted with the arrangements and the accommodations at the camp. We all had an enjoyable time there.

We left one evening at about eleven o'clock for a fine flight to San Francisco. Eisenhower called me shortly before we got in to say he wanted no word of his presence given out, that we would only stay long enough to refuel. He wanted a suggestion on a place where we could deplane with no excitement or speeches. I mentioned our depot at Oklahoma City as an out-of-the-way spot which had excellent accommodations, and I was sure he would not be bothered by anything. He said, "That sounds good. We will go there and stay there tonight." I hastened up front to give this word to the pilot.

I sent a confidential message to General Fritz Borum, who had charge of the Oklahoma City Air Materiel Area, and told him I was bringing a VIP into his place with no publicity, and all we would need was dinner and a place to sleep. Fritz Borum did a beautiful job of taking care of us. About eight o'clock he came to our quarters and explained to General Eisenhower that he had no troops here, except a few detachments of boarders, and that the great majority of his personnel were civilians who were having a dance that night. He knew they would appreciate it very much if Ike would make an appearance for a few minutes. "No one knows that you are here, so if you do not feel like making a short appearance, no one will be disappointed, but it would really make an occasion of it if you would show for a few minutes." Ike said yes, he would go, but no speeches or anything else. The crowd nearly went crazy when he came in and sat down at a table. He stayed for about fifteen minutes and then left for his quarters. Borum thanked him for his consideration and said good night. Knowing how General Eisenhower felt about such things, I also told him I thought it was a mighty fine gesture.

XXXIV

1946-47: Commanding General, Alaskan Department

✪ IN JUNE, 1946, Ed Hull returned one morning from a meeting in the Chief of Staff's office and told me I was being assigned as Commanding General of the Alaskan Department and he was going to Hawaii to take command there. I received this news with a good deal of uncertainty. I knew practically nothing about Alaska and, as it turned out, neither did anyone else in the Pentagon.

A few nights after I had received the news of my new assignment, we were having dinner with General and Mrs. Harold L. George in the Fort Myer Officers Club, when, by remarkable coincidence, General Delos C. Emmons, the Commanding General of the Alaskan Department came in. I asked him to sit with us. In reply to my question about what Alaska was like, he described it as awful, the end of the line. Evangeline asked him what we should take up there, and he said everything, and this we did, even to taking washtubs and scrubbing boards. Emmon's report on Alaska was very discouraging.

Several weeks later, we departed for our new station. On arrival in Seattle, we went to a hotel and the next day I checked in with the Alaskan Department's liaison officer who had made reservations for us on the airline to Juneau. At Juneau, General Hamp Atkinson, the C.G. of the Alaskan Air Command, met me with a B-17 to take us to Anchorage. I wanted to make a courtesy call on the Governor of the Territory, so we took a cab from the Juneau airport to the Governor's mansion. He was not at home, but we left our cards with his secretary, who happened to be at the house, and returned to the airport, where without delay we took off for Anchorage. Upon arrival we were met by Chief of Staff, an Army brigadier general, and some of the staff, including Colonel Hammond M. Monroe, another Leavenworth classmate.

We were taken to the house where Emmons lived, which was next door to the Chief of Staff's house. His family was not with him, and neither were the families of the majority of the officers. It was only under exceptional circumstances that Emmons permitted any of the families to come to Alaska, and then only those of the most senior officers. Emmons' house was bare, with nothing but issue furniture and one big easy chair with its upholstery worn and shiny from long use. One thing that fascinated me was the huge library of paperbacks. It was easy to see where Emmons spent most of his time.

The Acting Commander, Brig. Gen. Bathurse took me on a tour of the Post. Departmental HQ consisted of a number of outsized Quonset huts strung together. Here I came across Hammond Monroe of my Leavenworth class, now a colonel and serving as G-3. I decided to make him my Chief of Staff and it was a decision I never regreted.

Our next stop was Alaskan Air Command HQ with Brig. Gen. J. H. Atkinson in command. The Command had one station on the Aleutian island of Adak. Two more stations were located at Ladd Field in Fairbanks — a cold weather testing station with no air units — and another at Nome, used for refueling and also having no air units assigned.

I visited mess facilities, the movie theater, and the Post Hospital and the next day flew up to Ladd Field, commanded by Col. Louis Merrick, formerly of Bolling Field, D.C. This airdrome had been built with the idea of avoiding work stoppages due to cold weather (in winter the temperature often dropped to −40°) and tunnels had been constructed under the entire working area of the post. Although dug in the permafrost, they worked beautifully.

At Nome I had the commander show me arround and give me a list of complaints. He was very dissatisfied with his assignment. For one thing, he was a flying officer and had no airplane; for another he could not bring his family to the post, there being no facilities for dependents. I sympathized with him and was later able to obtain his relief, putting a bachelor, nonflying officer in command.

Adak, a very busy place during the Japanese occupation of Kiska and Attu, was noted for its bad weather, wind and fog. The post was commanded by Brig. Gen. E. C. Lynch, whom I had known at Randolph Field, and he had the situation well in hand. He had a fighter squadron under his command and said he had been cooperating with the U.S. International Air Lines flying from the U.S. to Japan. He also supported the small detachments we had on the island of Amchitka and Cold Bay since Adak had a huge supply depot fully stocked with repair parts and spares, mostly for Army vehicles and equipment.

Our next stop was Shemya Island, which had a landing field like a large carrier — long, narrow and smooth. Despite having no dock, three companies of trained Negro stevedores were stationed there. It was impossible to construct a loading dock because of the violent storms raging over this area, and the island commander had just about run out of ideas for keeping the stevedores busy.

By now I had a pretty solid idea of what the command consisted and I felt the outlying stations needed constant visits and inspections, particularly by members of my staff. This we arranged and I emphasized that the purpose of these visits was not to find fault but to help the post commanders do their job. Soon almost every air transport en route to the islands had members of my staff aboard.

One name I never saw on the loading lists was my senior chaplain and to my surprise he said it was not necessary for him to visit the islands and if he had to go by air he wished to be placed on flying status. We had quite a hassle over his attitude, which finally ended with my ordering him to make a visit to the Aleutians on the next transport leaving Elmendorf Field.

Another decision I made was to bring the fighter squadron from Adak into Elmendorf. My predecessor, Delos Emmons, had warned me that the squadron ought to remain at Adak despite the local pressure to move it into Anchorage. After a meeting with Hamp Atkinson, Lynch, and Brig. General Frank Everest, whom I assigned to Ladd Field in Fairbanks, we could find no good reason for keeping the squadron at Adak. I never regretted moving it; in fact, the weather at Elmendorf was so much better that Atkinson worked up a training schedule which improved the squadron's efficiency considerably.

"TASK FORCE FRIGID" from the 2nd Division at Fort Lewis, Washington, arrived by Army transport at Whittier, an Army post on the Kenai Peninsula — a grim place where the sides of the mountains rise straight up for several thousand feet on each side of the channel. The Task Force, composed of infantry, artillery and armored units, had to exercise to test equipment in sub-zero weather and also to teach troops to function under frigid conditions. I met the Task Force at Whittier and later returned as they loaded aboard the train to take them to Ladd Field. The operation was very successful, the troops operating in temperatures which plummeted as low as −50° F. There were a number of civilian specialists with the Task Force, among them Sir Hubert Wilkins who helped evaluate cold weather clothing gear, and food.

The vast territory of Alaska badly needed a War Plan — at least a delegation of responsibilities — and I put Atkinson in charge of developing one. His plan had the Navy responsible for the Aleutian Islands; Everest of Ladd Field responsible for the area north of the Yukon River; and the Alaskan Air Command responsible for the remainder of the Territory. After we arrived at what we thought were reasonable missions for the Navy, I took the plan over to Kodiak Island and presented it to the Admiral and his staff. The Admiral thought the plan right and reasonable but said he had no forces to implement it. This I understood and asked him to use the plan in operating what forces he had. We continued improving the plan during the winter and spring.

In the late spring of 1946 I received a message from the Air Force aide to the President saying Mr. Truman planned to visit Alaska in June. I was to keep this message confidential, for the President did not wish to make public appearances or speeches and wanted instead to find a good fishing spot where he and three or four political friends could relax. He was to arrive by Navy cruiser, docking at Anchorage.

I wired General George J. Richards, the Army Comptroller, for $50,000 to build a cabin, furnish it and build a road to it wherever it would be located. Next I called on my old friend, the Fish and Game Commissioner in Juneau, took him into my confidence and asked him where we could establish this special camp. He suggested Lake Louise and in a few days we drove up the highway toward Fairbanks until

we reached a trail which wound off through the woods. After walking
a mile or so we came out on a flat, located on the lakeside with snow
covered mountains in the distance, a beautiful and idyllic spot.

One day while construction men were building the access road necessary for this location, a reporter from an Anchorage newspaper, an
ex-GI who pictured himself another Drew Pearson, stopped one of the
workmen and asked what was going on. The soldier told the reporter
that the road was part of a cabin setup for General Craig. The news-
man took some photographs and soon had in his paper a story carrying
a headline about "Craig's Lovenest." Everyone on the post wanted to
know more about it by now — including my dear wife.

The excitement finally died down without a leak regarding the real
purpose of the cabin and, in my case, a radiogram from San Francisco
notified me the President had decided to cancel his proposed Alaskan
trip.

Not long after this, I received another message from Washington
notifying me that General Eisenhower, Chief of Staff of the Army,
would be coming to Alaska for a visit with five other people. I planned
to take him around the territory to Nome, Barrow, Adak, and then to
a fishing camp we had established at Naknek, in addition to a complete
inspection of Fort Richardson and Ladd Field. I hoped too to take the
Eisenhower party to Lake Louise for R & R.

Shortly after Ike's arrival, the Chamber of Commerce invited him
to a dinner in Anchorage, and in introducing him I said, simply: "Gentlemen, the Chief of Staff of the Army, General Eisenhower." Ike
looked at me in surprise for a moment but I think he liked the short
version rather than the long-winded recitation of his accomplishments
that so many, including Ike, had heard before.

Ike fell in love with Lake Louise and to prove it he spent four nights
there. We had a good cook and good food and the Eisenhower party
played bridge almost continually during the four days.

The General talked to all the men stationed at Ladd, visited a hospital there (and took exception to a soldier with venereal disease being
in bed instead of out working), visited the University of Alaska, and
gave a fine address to the Fairbanks Chamber of Commerce. At Barrow he talked to Navy oil contractors; at Nome he received a briefing

and was presented with a beautiful piece of carved walrus ivory; and the next day we flew to Naknek to our fishing camp.

After Ike returned to Washington I received a letter from him thanking me for arranging one of the finest inspection-fishing tours he had ever enjoyed.

About a week after Ike's departure, I received notice that a Committee of Congress, accompanied by some metropolitan newspaper reporters, would soon arrive at Ladd Field on an inspection tour. The chairman of this subcommittee were Congressmen Dewey Short of Missouri and his deputy John Sheridan of Philadelphia.

The chairman suffered a profuse nosebleed on the flight to Fairbanks and the white suit he wore was covered with blood, but he insisted on inspecting the guard of honor we had arranged for the party. We gave the committee members a briefing on our mission, the location of our stations in the Territory, and then suggested they proceed on down to Fort Richardson where I had made arrangements to put them up.

The newsmen were not present for the briefing inasmuch as some confidential material was included. At Richardson, I gave them a special briefing, explaining the military history of the Territory and our particular functions there. I asked that this information be treated off the record but most of the reporters sent in a story containing almost all my remarks. I became acquainted with Jack Sheridan, a friendship which has lasted to this day. *The Saturday Evening Post* published a complete article on the tour in which I was described as "a youngish man, with large brown eyes, who looked as though he was overcome by his responsibilities."

We had many visitors during the summer of 1947, something which made the Alaskan venture enjoyable. Among them were General and Mrs. Arnold, General Spaatz, General Elwood Quesada, General Handy, the Governor of the Territory, the Secretary of Interior and several admirals from Honolulu.

In late September I received a telephone call from General Vandenburg in Washington informing me I was being ordered back to Washington and promoted to Lieutenant General.

XXXV

1948-49: Deputy Chief of Staff, Inspector General

V ANDENBURG INFORMED ME that my new assignment
was as Deputy Chief of Staff, Materiel. The new Air Force,
as "Santa" Fairchild (now Vice Chief of Staff with my man
McKee as Assistant Vice Chief) explained to me had four deputy
chiefs: Lt. Gen. Idwal Edwards for Personnel, Gen. Lauris Norstad for
Operations, Lt. Gen. Howard Craig for Materiel, and Gen. Edward
Rawlings, Comptroller. Each deputy had full authority to take action
within the range of his responsibility and the deputies formed the Air
Force Council which met each morning to discuss decisions to be made
affecting the entire Air Force.

In my branch, I had a number of section chiefs — Lt. Gen. Lawrence
Craigie, in Aircraft and Engines; Gen. Curtis LeMay, Research and
Development; Lt. Gen. William Kepner, Nuclear Power; Lt. Gen.
Donald Putt, Missiles; Maj. Gen. Lyman Whitten, Supply and Ser-
vices; Maj. Gen. Robert Kauch, Air Installations.

I soon attended my first Air Council meeting in which Fairchild
served as Chairman, running the meetings with a firm hand. The purpose of the Council was to take some of the load off the shoulders of
the Chief of Staff and the Secretary, making policy decisions where appropriate or recommendations to the C.A.S. or Secretary.

One question I recall clearly was the matter of continuation of the
production of the B-36. General George Kenney, then in command of
the Strategic Air Forces, did not favor the B-36 and recommended construction of it be discontinued. I think Norstad agreed with him. Generals McNarney, C.G. of the Materiel Command at Dayton, and Kenneth Wolfe, also from Dayton, attended this meeting in defense of the
B-36. There were several stormy sessions on the subject, with the Navy

entering the fray opposing the airplane and the allocation of money toward its production. We finally approved the hundred B-36s scheduled for production and thought the matter settled. But the Navy, dissatisfied, finally convinced the Armed Forces Committee of Congress to investigate the matter. This session became known as "the Revolt of the Admirals." At the hearings it was revealed that the decision to continue production of B-36s was made by the Air Force Senior Officer's Board. I think many Congressmen thought Secretary Stuart Symington had pressured to continue the production but it was proven he had nothing to do with the decision.

About this time I learned that no member of the Board had flown the B-36 and I suggested that before the Congressional Committee hearings took place, we go down to Fort Worth and fly the airplane. Much to my surprise, the company test pilot put me in the pilot's seat and told me to take her off. This was a new experience for me but after some ragged taxiing to the end of the runway, we took off. The six-lever throttle was made too wide for my hand, but eventually I got all six engines opened up and we were in the air. Our flight was scheduled to go over Eglin Field, let out a gunnery target at 15,000 feet and fly several courses up and down the beach while fighter airplanes took turns firing at the target. After an hour of this, we turned toward Fort Worth and by the time we returned it had become dark. I wondered if the test pilot wanted me to make the night landing and I soon discovered he intended this. I started an approach at the runway, expecting the company pilot to take over any moment, but he did not. With some coaching from him, we landed and he congratulated me on a good flight.

The hearings of the Congressional Committee on the B-36 were exciting and the Committee Room crowded every session. The Air Force was vindicated by the investigation.

Mr. Arthur Barrows (Undersecretary of the Air Force) wanted to visit some Air Force installations and manufacturers on the West Coast and consulted with executive officers of several such companies before we embarked. From Boeing in Seattle we flew to Spokane to see the new B-47, a jet bomber which was to replace the B-36. The airplane which we inspected was a YB-47, the first one produced, and the company pilot invited me to take a ride in it. I liked it immensely. Curt LeMay at this time had taken over SAC and soon his people were working on the B-47 although eventually he turned it down as lacking the necessary range. But the B-47s that were built served many useful purposes such as reconnaissance and photography, using the famous airborne refueling technique.

In the summer of 1948 I went on leave for two weeks and accepted Malcolm Moss's invitation to attend the Bohemian Grove north of San Francisco — an activity of the renowned Bohemian Club. On our way up from Crissy Field (named for my old Commandant at Princeton) we stopped to see Gen. Arnold at his home in Sonoma. He was very happy to see us and took us on a tour of his place, all the while castigating his publishers for editing almost half of his book. "And you, Craig," he said unhappily, "wound up on the cutting-room floor."

Our stay at Bohemian Grove was very pleasant. Supreme Court Justice Bob Jackson was a member of our camp and I became well acquainted him. Here also I met former President Herbert Hoover and again General Mark Clark. About the time I was to return to Washington, I met Ambassador Richard Patterson, our representative in Yugoslavia who was returning to New York. I invited him to join me in flying to Washington and he accepted. During our conversation on the way back, he asked me if any major problems had come up in the new Air Force and this question led me to explain my difficult situation with Secretary Symington.

The Secretary had a habit of calling General McNarney of Dayton on the phone and giving him instructions with regard to the purchase of airplanes, spare parts, engines and equipment of all sorts. Fortunately, Joe McNarney told me about this, promising to call me back and tell me of the instructions he received. I protested to Symington about this procedure, saying I was his contact on all materiel matters and if he wanted to relay any instructions about materiel to anyone to call me direct. Symington, hotly disagreeing with me, said he felt he could call anyone in the Air Force and give them instructions. I said that he was right, but if he would only let me know when he contacted McNarney, everything would be much better. The Secretary eventually passed more of his instructions through my office.

One of my jobs as Deputy for Materiel was to sit on a Board which allocated facilities and supplies to the Air Force from the Army. The Chief of Staff was anxious to get the Air Force into the blue uniform. The separation of the Air Force from the Army had caught the Quartermaster General by surprise. He had already obligated his uniform money, buying the Air Force the Army uniform and having no funds for the purchase of blue uniforms. Mr. Barrows came to the rescue here, due to his knowledge and experience at Sears, and found that while the QMG had allocated the funds, this was purely an interoffice transaction and the funds had not been obligated. A switch was made from olive drab to blue when purchasing the materials for manufacture.

In the summer of 1949, I was transferred from Deputy for Materiel to Inspector General of the Air Force, replacing General Hugh Knerr, who had retired. I talked to General Vandenburg whether my work as DCSM had been satisfactory. He replied, "Hell yes — but I need you now as I.G." When I asked him what the problems were he said, "Everything."

This was a job I learned to like. It put to use the experience of all my years of service and there was much to learn. The IG office had a very simple organization: an Executive Office, an Assistant IG in charge of Special investigations, and an Air Police (Enforcement) Office. Special Investigations was headed by Reserve Brigadier General Joseph F. Carroll, a former F.B.I. official who was secured for us by Secretary Symington — one of the smartest things he did for the Air Force. Joe was a wonderful person, good-looking, smart and familiar with the ways of Washington. He organized a school for investigators in Washington and then started a very careful recruitment campaign for operatives. The school had just been stabilized as far as facilities, curriculum, staff and student body when I arrived on the scene. He used graduates to establish a section at each Air Force Base in the United States and overseas.

XXXVI

1950-55 : War College, Inter-American Defense Board, Retirement

⭐ GENERAL VANDENBURG WAS DISSATISFIED with the way aircraft accident investigation, under the supervision of the Deputy for Operations, was running. He said he was tired of appearing before Committees of Congress to explain the cause of accidents, only to discover the Congressmen knew more about the cases than he did. He wanted all accidents and their causes reported immediately to him and told me to take over the project.

Col. John W. "Willie" Persons, head of Accident Investigation, had his office at Langley and I asked him to come up to Washington. I had known him when we were stationed at the Tactical School at Montgomery, Alabama, and now recruited him to help me.

Another "recruit" was Major General Victor Bertrandias, an old friend who had just returned from a command in the Southwest Pacific, intending to return to civilian life until convinced I needed him. Bertrandias, an excellent pilot himself, disputed what past accident records indicated — that most such accidents were attributable to "pilot error," and asked to be placed as a "tenant" at some Air Force installation on the West Coast to be near the important aircraft manufacturers. We found a place for him at the San Bernardino Depot.

While Bertrandias was getting settled at San Bernardino, we had another accident involving B-29s. A squadron of these planes were ordered to Bermuda from March AFB, flying in flights of three and separated by several minutes of time. One flight ditched in the ocean — all personnel being rescued. Willie Persons conducted an investigaiton of this incident and soon had a report on the desk of the Chief of Staff. One time, at least, when the Chief was called before a Congressional Committee, he came prepared with the full details and as a result instructions were sent to the SAC Commander to prevent a recurrence.

Gen. Curtis LeMay could not believe Persons' report and came charging into the Chief's office to protest. We got Willie up from Langley and he spread out the signed reports made by the rescued crewmen — which calmed LeMay considerably. Curt became one of the strongest supporters of the new Safety Program, by the way, and I liked the way Persons stood up against the protests of this great airman. I think LeMay was impressed too.

In 1953 I made a delightful trip to Europe — traveling with my aide Col. Fred Prasse and our wives to Germany, Austria, Rome (where we had an audience with Pope Pius XII), Paris and London. When I returned, Bertrandias — in charge of our flying safety program — said General LeMay was supporting us 100% and that our investigative procedures in flying accidents were making a terrific impact on the whole Air Force.

In attending a cocktail party given by the French Mission, shortly after my return from Europe, a French Air Force officer approached me and asked if I were not General Craig. "You don't remember me?" he said, and I had to admit that I did not. He said he had been a member of the P-40 squadron which was under my command at Thelepte in North Africa and that he had been one of the officers I "decorated" with blank-paper diplomas in lieu of the U.S. Air Medal at Maison Blanche. He gave a big laugh and I said it had been one of my most embarrassing moments. My man told me he and his squadron mates had got quite a "keek" out of it and that the medals had been delivered the next day.

This French officer gave me some good advice when I brought up a matter of some concern to me — I wanted Vic Bertrandias considered for the French Legion of Honor and my cocktail party acquaintance advised me to write him a letter (he worked in the office of the French Ambassador), giving all of Bertrandias' background.

Bertrandias was born in France and came to the U.S. with his parents at a young age. As a young man he was interested in automobiles and auto racing and when the World War broke out he immediately enlisted in the Aviation Section of the U.S. Signal Corps and was sent to

Issoudoun in France where he met the then Lt. Eddie Rickenbacker. Bertrandias learned to fly in France and after the war resigned his commission to work for Donald Douglas as an aircraft salesman. He was sent to China and became very successful, living in the Far East nearly twenty years, accumulating Douglas stock and probably considerable wealth. When World War II broke out he returned to the U.S. Air Service, serving with distinction.

Some months after sending Bertrandias' dossier to the French Ambassador, Vic appeared in my office to show me the Legion of Honor and Croix de Guerre which had been awarded him at one of the French air bases nera Paris — the French sparing nothing in their ceremony.

I hastily wrote a note to my friend in the French Embassy thanking him and telling him that nothing could have brought more joy to this fine man.

Not long afterwards, Bertrandias retired and in a big farewell review at San Bernardino, I pinned the Distinguished Service Medal on his chest. He died about a year later on his small ranch in San Fernando Valley, having made a great contribution to the Air Force.

Another of our great men, General Muir "Santa" Fairchild died at about this time. Hoyt Vandenberg had received the applause of the miltiary aviation world when he nominated Fairchild to the four-starred post of Vice-Chief. He had built the Air University following World War II, using the Air War College, the Air Command and Staff College and the Squadron Officer's School as the building blocks.

During the winter of 1950-51 I had a very unusual experience — one of the strangest episodes in my memory. A colonel came to my office (we will call him "Colonel A"), a tall, handsome fellow with his chest literally covered with ribbons. He had a story to tell me.

Back in 1939 he was a junior student at the University of California at Berkeley, rooming with another young fellow whom we will call "B." "A" decided, what with war clearly on the horizon, that he wanted to be a pilot. A recruiting office gave him all the information he needed to become a flying cadet and he found that his marks in school, if above a certain level, would exempt him from examinations. Because he had only average marks he feared he would have to take the chance of failing these examinations. His roommate "B" however was an outstanding student and so "A" went to the university's "B's" transcript, explaining he was applying for an Army commission. The clerk readily prepared this paper and "A" took a further step: he had to have two letters of recommendation on his moral character, so he devised the names of a minister and banker in Reno, Nevada ("B's" hometown) and prepared the letters. Next, the intricate scheme became even more complex; he wrote to "B's" place of birth, obtained a birth certificate, and filled it out.

Soon "A" was told to report before an examining board at Hamilton Field, California, where he was exempted from all examinations except the physical, and within a few weeks was sent on to Randolph Field for flying training. Throughout all this, "A" used "B's" name and credentials. He had no trouble with his flying and soon graduated as a 2nd Lieutenant. After some stateside service, he became a flight commander, a 1st lieutenant in a fighter group headed overseas.

"A" (still using "B's" name and history) flew nearly a hundred combat missions in Europe and by the end of the war had risen to the rank of colonel and a group commander with an outstanding record. While in England he married and had brought his wife back to the States. The couple had three children — all known by "B's" name, of course. He had graduated from the Air War College and now had duty in Plans and Operations Division.

More and more he had been stricken by his fraudulent identity and could no longer sleep at night, fearing the consequences if the scheme fell apart. He had never mentioned the affair to a soul, not even his wife, until he came to me.

My first reaction, after hearing this incredible tale, was simply to assure the man I would look into it. I thought the Secretary of the Air Force's Board for the Correction of Military Records would be the final authority, but felt I would have to talk to the Deputy for Personnel, General Idwal Edwards, to get the tangle unraveled. In the meantime, I told "A" to return to duty and say nothing until he heard from me.

After obtaining his 201-File, I found, as expected, his records inextricably mixed up. I learned that "A's" namesake — "B" — had gotten an Army commission himself and had been assigned to the Sixth Army in the Pacific. He had been seriously wounded in the Philippines and even now was confined at Letterman Army Hospital in San Francisco. Separating the papers on the two men, I took "B's" to the Army Adjutant General, then moved to present the case to the Board for the Correction of Records.

At first the members of the Board were furious at this deception but General Edwards of Personnel took the point of view that the only reason for the fraud had been "A's" eagerness to be accepted as a flying cadet and that as a result of this, the man had compiled a thoroughly fine record. Finally it was decided that a reprimand would suffice as punishment.

"A" had to go to court to make his name change (back to the original) legal and official.

I believe the Board's decision was correct and the decision pleased me very much.

EARLY IN THE SUMMER OF 1952, Major General Bryant Boatner — the Secretary of the Air Staff — replaced me as Inspector General. Van notified me I would become Commandant of the National War College; I protested that I was not sufficiently qualified for the job, but to no avail. Vandenberg expressed confidence in me and I said I would do my best.

I soon had a visit at Fort McNair with Lt. Gen. Harold R. "Pinkie" Bull of the Army, present Commandant of the War College. I had known him from my days on the W.D. General Staff and on Ike's staff in North Africa. He assured me I would enjoy the job.

In order to have a better idea of what students faced at the College, I took the entire course myself. It was not easy but was certainly worth the effort.

During the winter of 1952, Major General Robert "Bob" Walsh asked me to consider taking the Chairmanship of the Inter-American Defense Board — a group composed of senior representatives of our Latin American neighbor's military forces. Bob himself currently held the chairmanship of this important group which had been organized early in World War II when Germany was making inroads in all of Latin America.

Bob Walsh's son, "Pete," just returned from a tour of duty in Korea as a bomber navigator, served as my aide during most of my tour of duty at the War College and was a fine young man.

The Inter-American Defense Board proved a very interesting assignment and its social affairs put Evangeline and me on another circuit of the Washington party-givers — the diplomatic people of Latin America.

As Commandant of the War College, I noticed what I considered a decided decline in the quality of students being enrolled and after observing this factor for a time, I wrote a letter to the Joint Chiefs, under whom the college functioned, suggesting that admission requirements be prescribed including the stipulations that students be full colonels or captains of the Navy with equivalent rank for civilians; that the military students be graduates of their own service war college and that they fit into a prescribed age-service group so that the government could obtain some return on their investment in this period of their education. I suggested too that the National War College not be used as a substitute for the service war college education and that graduates be used on higher staffs such as those of the Chiefs of a military service, the JCS, the military committee of the UN and NATO. These, I said, were the jobs for which our students were being trained.

This letter was processed down to a Lieutenant Colonel, a JCS staff officer who was not a graduate of the War College nor one knowing or caring about it. He recommended no change after his "investigation."

During the winter, I decided to make a visit to all the countries represented on the Inter-American Defense Board and, in two years, visited Rio de Janeiro, Buenos Aires, Santiago, and Lima; Cuba, Haiti and the Dominican Republic, Mexico City, Guatemala, San Salvador, Honduras, Nicaragua, Columbia, and Venezuela. I believe the visits increased the prestige of the Board in the eyes of each member government. I was able to get a group of War College students launched on a similar South and Central American trip, took members of the Board on tours of the War College — with appropriate briefings — and this combination of events probably led, at least partially, to the establishment of a Latin-American school at Ft. McNair a few years later.

Upon my relief from the Board early in June 1955, I made a farewell speech which I think was the best of my career.

On graduation day at the War College, the principal speaker was Secretary of Defense Charles Wilson who was very gracious in his remarks. After the ceremonies in the auditorium, several students and faculty members waylaid me and presented me with a plaque with the College's coat-of-arms. In receiving this gift, I said it was "my diploma and the heaviest one I had ever received." I promised to keep it in a place of prominence in my home provided they would give a similar plaque to General Bull and Admiral Harry Hill, my predecessors.

In leaving Ft. McNair to retirement on June 15, 1955, I put in a call to Tommy White, the Chief of Staff, to say good-bye to him, and he said he would be seeing me on the 30th at the Review. He said he supposed I knew that the Chief of Staff would pin my 3rd DSM on me during that review. I did not know about it and told Tommy I was absolutely exhausted and did not think I could go through with the ceremony.

Needless to say I never received that DSM. It did not seem important at the time, but as the years roll on I want it more and more.

I suppose my thinking on it is similar to my reflections on the whole series of events, a lifetime of events, which began when a twelve-year-old boy went down to the beach at Atlantic City and saw a man in a checkered cap. . . .

To Pinky Craig – with admiration for his ability as a soldier and gratitude for his loyal and efficient support and assistance in World War II.

Dwight D. Eisenhower

APPENDICES

APPENDIX I

ANDERSON, Sir Kenneth A. (1891 - 1959). Commanding General, British First Army, 1942.

ARNOLD, Henry H. "Hap" (1886 - 1950). Chief of U.S. Army Air Corps, 1938; Chief of U.S. Air Force, 1941; General of the Army, 1944; General of the Air Force, 1949. "Hap" was short for "Happy," describing his nature.

ATKINSON, J. H. "Hamp" (1900 - 1971). Commanding General, Alaskan Air Command, 1946.

BALCHEN, Bernt (1899 - 1973). Norwegian-American Arctic explorer and Air Force officer.

BOURKE-WHITE, Margaret (1906 - 1971). Staff photographer *Time - Life*, and author.

BROOKE, Sir Alan F., First Viscount Alanbrooke (1883 - 1963). Commanding General, British Second Army Corps, 1939 - 40; C-in-C, Home Forces, 1940 - 41; Chief, Imperial General Staff, 1941; Field Marshal, 1944.

BROOKINS, Walter Dubois (1890 - 1953). Pioneer aviator, student of the Wrights; made first flight on 28 March 1910 and soloed after two and a half hours instruction. Retired from flying in 1914 and became partner in the Davis-Brookins Aircraft Co. of Hollywood, Calif. He died in Los Angeles on 29 April, 1953. "Flying is inherently safe," Brookins always said, "but it is mercilessly unforgiving of human error."

BYRNES, James F. (1879 - 1973). Former Congressman and Senator and Associate Justice of the U.S. Supreme Court, served as Director of the Office of Economic Stabilization, 1942 - 43; Director of War Mobilization, 1943- 45; Secretary of State, 1945 - 47. Later Governor of South Carolina.

CHENNAULT, Claire L. (1890 - 1958). Air advisor to Generalissimo Chiang Kai-shek, forming volunteer air corps ("Flying Tigers") in 1937; widely acclaimed for protecting the Burma Road against superior Japanese air strength, 1941. Resigned from U.S. Army in 1945 as Major General.

CLARK, Mark W. (1896 -   ). Commander, Fifth Army in North Africa and Italy, 1943 - 44; secret envoy landed by submarine at Algiers in 1942 to urge French leaders to join the Allies.

CONINGHAM, Sir Arthur (1895 - 1965). Commanded British and American air forces in North Africa, 1943. From service with New Zealanders in WWI, gained nickname "Maori," inevitably changed to "Mary."

CRISSY, Dana H. (d. 1919). West Point, 1909; Commandant, School of Aeronautics, Princeton University, 1917 - 18; died in air crash in Utah on 8 October 1919.

CURTISS, Glenn H. (1878 - 1930). American pioneer aviation inventor, flyer.

DARLAN, Jean Louis Xavier Francois (1881 - 1942). French Admiral of the Fleet; Vice Premier of France during Vichy Regime. C-in-C of all armed forces in North Africa before Anglo-American invasion, 1942; assassinated on 24 December 1942.

DOOLITTLE, James H. (1896 -   ). Led bombing raid over Tokyo, 1942; commanded U.S. air forces in North African invasion, 1942; Commanding General, Eighth Air Force, Europe, 1944.

EMMONS, Delos C. (1888 - 1965). Commanding General, U.S. Air Corps, 1940; Commander, Hawaiian Department, U.S. Army, 1941 - 43; CG, Alaskan Department, 1943 - 46.

FAIRCHILD, Muir S. "Santa" (1894 - 1950). Vice Chief of Staff, U.S. Air Force 1947 - 53; Commandant, Air University, 1945 - 47; trained to fly on Caproni bombers in Italy during WWI.

FREDENALL, Lloyd R. (1883 - 1963). Led U.S. II Corps landing at Oran and Algiers, 1942, first combat jump of U.S. paratroopers. Retired in 1946 as Lt. General.

GEORGE, Harold L. (1893 -   ). Entered U.S. Aviation Signal Corps in 1917 and rose to Lt. General in 1944. Assistant Chief of Air Staff, Air Plans, 1941; Commanding General, Air Transport Command, Army Air Forces, 1942-46.

HANDY, Thomas T. (1892 -   ). Assistant Chief of Staff, Operations Division, 1944; Commanding General, Fourth Army, Texas, 1947; C-in-C, European Troops, 1949 - 52.

HOPKINS, Harry L. (1890 - 1946). U.S. Secretary of Commerce, 1938 - 40; head of Lend Lease, 1941; President Roosevelt's political envoy to Russia and Britain, 1941; special assistant to FDR, 1942-45. Churchill found Hopkins "the most faithful and perfect channel of communication" between himself and FDR and paid tribute to "the priceless work of Hopkins. . . . a soul that flamed out of a frail and failing body."

HULL, John Edwin "Ed" (1895-   ). In Army career between 1917-51, rose from 2nd Lt. to General. Vice Chief of Staff, U.S. Army, 1951-53.

ISMAY, Sir Hastings L., First Baron Ismay (1887-1965). Nicknamed "Pug," Ismay served as Chief of Staff to Churchill in WW2 and liaison between the PM and Eisenhower. Secretary-General, NATO, 1952-57.

KING, Ernest J. (1878-1956). As midshipman-cadet from Annapolis, served in Santiago, Cuba, in Spanish-American War, 1898; C-in-C, Atlantic Fleet, 1940; Admiral, 1941; Chief of Naval Operations, 1942-45; Admiral of the Fleet, 1944.

LEMAY, Curtis (1906-   ). Commander of Marianas-based 21st Bomber Command which carried A-bombs to Japan. C-in-C, Strategic Air Command, 1948-57; Air Force Chief of Staff, 1961-64.

LEMNITZER, Lyman L. (1892-   ). War Plans Division, War Department General Staff, 1941; CG, Allied Forces, England, 1942; European duty, 1942-45; CG, 7th Infantry Division, Korea, 1951-52; CG, Far East Command, 1955; Army Vice Chief of Staff, 1957-59; Army Chief of Staff, 1959-60; Chairman, Joint Chiefs of Staff, 1960-62; Supreme Allied Commander, Europe, 1963-69.

MARSHALL, George C. (1880-1959). Chief of Staff, U.S. Army, 1939-45; General of the Army, 1944. U.S. Ambassador to China, 1945-47; Secretary of State, 1947-49; Secretary of Defense, 1950-51. Originator of Marshall Plan; awarded Nobel Peace Prize, 1953.

MILLING, Thomas DeWitt (1887-1960). American pioneer aviator. Learned to fly with Wright Brothers in 1911.

MITCHELL, William "Billy" (1879-1936). Born in Nice, France; served in Spanish-American War, Philippine Insurrection, Mexican Border; Commander of American air forces in American Expeditionary Force, 1917-18; court-martialed for insubordination for criticism of War and Navy Departments for mismanagement of aviation service, 1925. Convicted and sentenced to suspension from service for five years. Resigned, 1926.

MONTGOMERY, Sir Bernard Law, First Viscount Montgomery of Alamein (1887-   ). Divisional commander in France 1939-40; CG, British 8th Army, Egypt, 1942; victor at El Alamein, 1943; CG, Allied Armies, Northern France, 1944; Chief of Imperial General Staff, 1946.

MOUNTBATTEN, Louis, First Earl Mountbatten of Burma (1900-   ). Great grandson of Queen Victoria; Chief of British Combined Operations (Commandos), 1942; Supreme Allied Commander, Southeast Asia, 1943-46.

PATTON, George S. (1885-1945). CG, U.S. Forces, Morocco, 1942; CG, Second Army Corps, Tunisia, 1943; CG, Seventh Army, Sicily, 1943; CG, Third Army, Western Europe, 1944-45.

PORTAL, Sir Charles Frederick Algernon, First Viscount Portal of Hungerford (1893-1971). Chief of British Air Staff, 1940-45; had major role in the important allied conferences as the air member of the Chief of Staff's Committee under chairmanship of Sir Alan Brooke.

POUND, Sir Dudley Pickman Rogers (1877-1943). First Sea Lord and Chief of British Naval Staff, 1939-43. "To him, more than any other, must go credit for the change of fortune at sea by 1943," says one source. Pound died a few weeks after resigning as First Sea Lord, on 21 October 1943 — Trafalgar Day.

RICHARDSON, Tracy (1892-1949). American soldier-of-fortune.

ROOSEVELT, Elliott (1910-   ). Third child of FDR and Eleanor, Col. Roosevelt flew P-38 reconnaissance missions in North Africa in 1942, and by the end of the war was promoted Brigadier General.

SANDERS, Sir Arthur Penrose Martyn (1898-   ). British Air Chief Marshal; Director of Ground Defense, Air Ministry, 1940-42; Chief of Air Section, Air Force HQ, London, 1943-50; Vice Chief of Air Staff, 1948-50.

SHEEAN, James Vincent (1899-   ). American foreign correspondent perhaps best known for his book *An American Among the Riffi* (1926).

SHERMAN, Forrest (1896-1951). Commanded U.S.S. Wasp, 1942; Deputy C-in-C, Pacific Ocean Areas, 1943; Deputy Chief of Naval Operations, 1946; Commander, Naval Forces, Mediterranean, 1948; Chief of Naval Operations, 1949.

SINCLAIR, Sir Archibald (1890-   ). British Secretary of State for Air, 1940-45.

SLESSOR, Sir John Cotesworth (1897-   ). British Chief Air Marshal. C-in-C, Royal Air Force, 1946. A foremost British Air Planner.

SMITH, Walter Bedell (1895-1961). First U.S. Secretary of Combined Chiefs of Staff, Great Britain and U.S.; later Eisenhower's Chief of Staff. Signed, with Germany's Jodl, the German surrender document. Worked up through ranks from private to General. Nicknamed "Beetle." Greatly admired by Churchill.

SPAATZ, Carl (1891-1974). Chief of Army Air Force in Europe, 1942; Deputy Allied Air Commander, Mediterranean, 1943; Chief, U.S. Bombing Force, Germany, 1944; Japan, 1945; nicknamed "Tooey." First commander of Eighth Air Force in Britain, 1942-43; took command for all U.S. air operations in North Africa, 1943; returned to England in 1944 to become first CG of U.S. Strategic Air Force (which included the 8th Air Force in England and the 15th in Italy). Shifted his HQ to the Marianas Islands in the Pacific where he directed the final phase of the American strategic bombardment of Japan. Became the first Chief of Staff of the U.S. Air Force, 1947.

STEFANSSON, Vilhjalmur (1879-1962). Canadian-born of Icelandic parents, Arctic explorer and author.

STIMSON, Henry L. (1867-1950). U. S. Secretary of War, 1911-13; served in Field Artillery in France in WWI; Governor-General, Philippines, 1927-29; Secretary of State, 1929-33; Secretary of War, 1940-45.

SUMMERALL, Charles P. (1867-1955). Commanded First Division of AEF in WWI; Chief of Staff, U.S. Army, 1926-30; retired in 1930 and became President of The Citadel.

TEDDER, Sir Arthur W., First Baron Tedder (1890-1967). British Air Chief Marshal; Deputy Commander, RAF, 1940-41; C-in-C, Middle East, 1940-41; Coordinated air activities in campaign which drove Rommel from Egypt and

Libya, 1942-43; Allied Air Commander-in-Chief, Mediterranean; Deputy Supreme Allied Commander, 1943-46; Chief of Air Staff, 1946-50.

TRUSCOTT, Lucian K. (1895-1965). Field deputy to Eisenhower in Tunisia, 1942-43; successful in smashing Germans at Anzio.

VANDENBERG, Hoyt (1899-1954). Chief of Staff, Northwest African Strategic Air Force, 1942-43; Commanding General, 9th Air Force in France and Germany, 1943-45; Chief of Staff, U.S. Air Force, 1948.

WEDEMEYER, Al (1897-   ). In 1944 succeeded Gen. Stillwell in command of the U.S. Army Forces, China.

WOOD, Leonard (1860-1927). Entered the army as a contract surgeon, won the Medal of Honor in the campaign against Geronimo, military governor of Cuba and Philippines, Chief of Staff U.S. Army.

Receiving the Distinguished Service Medal (with Oak Leaf Cluster) from General G. C. Marshall, March 12, 1945

APPENDIX II

AVRO. This British plane, 29'-6" long, wing span of 36', was powered by an 80 hp. Gnome engine and had a speed of from 75-80 mph. On November 21, 1914, three AVROs of the Royal Naval Air Service flew 125 miles from Belfort, France, to Fredrichshafen, Germany, and dropped twelve 20-pound bombs on zeppelin sheds and gas works there — the first long-distance bombing raid over hostile territory.

BEAU. The Beaufighter was a twin-engined RAF night interceptor fighter plane designed for use against German bombers as well as Axis shipping. It was equipped with four 20 mm. cannon; six .303-caliber machineguns; one 2,127 lb. torpedo or one 1,650 lb. torpedo; and two 250-lb. bombs or eight rocket projectiles. Flew 320 mph, range about 1,480 miles.

B-18. The standard U.S. medium bomber of the late 1930s; speed 167 mph, ceiling 25,850 feet, range 1,200 miles. Equipped with three .30 cal. machineguns. A six-place all-metal mid-wing monoplane, manufactured by Douglas and nicknamed "Bolo."

B-36. The last propeller-driven bomber of the U.S. Air Force, the backbone of the Strategic Air Command during the immediate post-WWII period. Immense range of 12,000 miles; huge bomb capacity; six pusher engines and remote-control air-to-air armament. The last model added jet pods to each wing for added speed.

B-47. First all-jet U.S. bomber, the Boeing "Stratojet," USAF swept-wing medium bomber. Top speed over 600 mph. First flight in 1947, replaced by B-52 in 1955.

BT-2. The basic observation plane from which this trainer was derived was the post-WWI replacement for the DeHavilland DH-4.

C-47. The famous Douglas DC-3 gone to war. Cargo and troop carrier; armed with .30 cal. and .50 cal. machineguns for defense. The C-47, the Garand Rifle, and the Jeep were said to be the three most valuable items of hardware the U.S. possessed in WWII.

DH-4. British-designed, American and British produced plane with either an eight-cylinder, 150 hp. Hispano-Suiza engine or 12-cylinder, 400 hp. Liberty engine. Wood frame, fabric-covered; 125 mph, ceiling 20,000 feet, range 325 miles (Liberty engine). Armed with two .30 machineguns. The DH-4 was the only U.S. quantity-produced combat plane of WWI.

FW-190. German Focke-Wulf fighter and one of the outstanding aircraft of the Second World War. Flew at 404 mph, armed with two 7.92 mm. machine-guns, four 20 mm. cannon. Outclassed the British Spitfire VB and the German Messerschmidt 109E.

JN4-D. Curtis manufactured machine with OX-5 engine.

JN4-H. Curtis manufactured, the "Hisso-Jenny" used the Hispano-Suiza engine 100-120 hp. Originally an advanced trainer, it became a primary trainer flown by Reserves and National Guard.

JN6-H. One of the last of the "Jenny" series used by the U.S. Army.

JU-88. The Junkers; most versatile aircraft in the Luftwaffe in WWII; level bomber, dive bomber, reconnaissance and night-fighter. No match for British Spitfire and Hurricanes during the Battle for Britain. Bombload 5,510 lbs., flew at 292 mph.

MB-2. Martin bomber. Equipped with two Liberty engines of 418 hp. each; 98 mph, ceiling 23,800 ft., bomb load 1,040 lbs. Equipped with five .30 cal. machineguns. A fabric-covered biplane, this modification of the original Martin was used in the historic bomber-battleship trials of July, 1921.

ME-109. Messerschmidt design, this German fighters was tested in combat in the Spanish Civil War. As fast as the British Spitfire but less manouverable. Outflew British Hurricane. 357 mph, equipped with two 7.9 mm. machineguns, two 20 mm. cannon.

NBS-1. A slightly improved MBE bomber (night bomber, short range, 1st model).

P-12. Fabric-covered biplane manufactured by Boeing; 500 hp. air-cooled engine, 182 mph, ceiling 27,900 ft., range 475 miles. Equipped with two .30 or .50 machineguns. The best Army acrobatic plane of 1930's. flown by Chennault and others in Air Shows.

P-38. Lockheed-manufactured "Lightning." Fastest (450 mph) U.S. fighter, doubled as bomber and reconnaissance plane. Introduced in North Africa against German and Italian aircraft. Equipped with one 20 mm. cannon and four .50 machineguns plus bomb and rocket capacity. The top U.S. ace of WWII, Richard I. Bong, scored 40 victories against the Japanese in the Pacific with the P-38.

P-39. The Bell-manufactured "Airacobra," this fighter was no match for the top Japanese and German planes. Equipped with one 37 mm. cannon, two .50 cal. machineguns in nose and four .30 cal. in wings.

P-40. The Curtis-manufactured "Warhawk," the P-40 formed 52 percent of U.S. fighter plane strength in December, 1941. Used by British, U.S., and Flying Tigers. 357 mph, equipped with two .50 cal. machineguns, and two .30s.

P-47. A massive, heavy U.S. fighter (nearly twice the weight of the RAF Spitfire), the P-47 successfully fought the best the Luftwaffe had to offer. Armoured and with eight .50 cal. machineguns, it could both take and dish out terrific punishment. 426 mph, nicknamed "Thunderbolt."

PT-1. Primary trainer which replaced the remaining JN4-DS used as trainers in 1927. Manufactured by Consolidated.

O'Donnell, Witten, Davies, Craig, Fitzmaurice, Baisley, Gibson, Henry
at Langley Field, 1939　　　　　　　　(U.S. Army Air Corps Photo)

EDITOR'S ACKNOWLEDGEMENTS

Special gratitude is extended to a number of people who are deeply interested in General Craig's book and who gave aid in a number of ways toward seeing his memoirs reach publication. These special people are:

MRS. ROSALIE CRAIG, wife of the General; Mrs. C. M. (Jeanne Craig) Stanfill, daughter of the General, and Dr. Stanfill, to whom his book is dedicated, for their graciousness, time and effort;

MR. JAMES B. MURRAY, U.S. Army retired, of El Paso; military historian and researcher who helped immeasurably in putting together the appendices for the book;

DR. E. H. ANTONE, DR. CARL HERTZOG, and members of the Editorial Board of Texas Western Press for their sustained interest;

DIANE DAVIDSON, niece of General Craig, who gave the first rough draft of the story its initial "cleansing," her efforts and time;

COL. PAUL A. ROCKWELL of Asheville, N.C., long-time and treasured friend who wrote the editor: "Indeed I do remember General 'Pinkie' Craig; I thought him by far the best of the young U.S. Air Force Generals who went into North Africa with us in 1942. Colonel Harold Willis and I used to chuckle at most of the other very young and entirely inexperienced USAF 'brass' who floundered considerably, but had great respect for 'Pinkie' Craig. He went right out in the field with the pilots, caught pneumonia at Thelepte, Tunisia, if I recall correctly, in December, 1942 or January, 1943, by sleeping on the cold, wet ground wrapped up in a blanket. This was in the mountains and bitterly cold. We feared for his life. I do not remember seeing him since but always think of him as a splendid officer and that rarest of all things in the modern world, an authentic gentleman and leader of soldiers."

JOHN PAUL JONES, the fine El Paso artist, whose contributions to General Craig's book went beyond those of an artistic nature;

As for Lieutenant General Howard Arnold Craig himself, let it be known that it has been a rare privilege knowing and working with this exemplary, modest man. He fits perfectly, without conscious effort, the description contained in the last twenty words of Col. Rockwell's recollection.

July 1, 1974   DALE L. WALKER

Ike and Craig in Alaska, 1947

Lauris Norstad   *Muir Fairchild*   *William McKee*

The first meeting of the Air Sta

dwall H. Edwards   Howard A. Craig   Edwin R. Rawlings

, Air Force, 1947

(U.S. Army Air Corps Photo)

Designed by

EVAN HAYWOOD ANTONE